Spiritual but Not Religious?

An Oar Stroke Closer to the Farther Shore

Reid B. Locklin

LITURGICAL PRESS
Collegeville, Minnesota

www.litpress.org

Cover design by Ann Blattner.

"Only Happy When It Rains"
by Doug Erikson, Shirley Manson, Steve Marker and Bryan Vig.
© 1995 Irving Music, Inc. on behalf of Itself and Vibecrusher Music and Almo Music
Corp. on behalf of itself and Deadarm Music (BMI/ASCAP).
All rights reserved. Used by permission.

The Scripture quotations contained herein are from the New Revised Standard Version
Bible, New Oxford Annotated Bible, © 1991, 1989, Division of Christian Education of
the National Council of the Churches of Christ in The United States of America, and are
used by permission. All rights reserved.

1   2   3   4   5   6   7   8

Library of Congress Cataloging-in-Publication Data

Locklin, Reid B.
    Spiritual but not religious? : an oar stroke closer to the farther shore / by Reid B.
Locklin.—1st ed.
        p. cm.
    Includes bibliographical references and index.
    ISBN 0-8146-3003-0
    1. Church. 2. Church membership. 3. Spirituality—Catholic Church. 4. Catholic
Church—Apologetic literature. 5. Hinduism—Relations—Catholic Church.
6. Catholic Church—Relations—Hinduism. 7. Locklin, Reid B. I. Title.

BX1746.L62   2004
248.4'82—dc22

                                                            2004006465

For Mom and Edge

Contents

Acknowledgments   vii

Introduction — Raising the Question   1
 The Professor   1
 Spiritual but Not Religious?   2
 A Moment of Recognition   5
 Teachers Along the Way   7
 Back to the Beginning   10

Chapter 1 — On Seekers   13
 The Priest   13
 A Moment of Clarity and Disgust   16
 Beautiful Garbage   21
 Split Down the Middle by Hope and Desire   24
 A Care Package from the Lord   27
 Gifts of Conversion   30
 Who We Are   34

Chapter 2 — On Teachers   37
 The Guru   37
 A First Hurdle   39
 Friendship and Fluency   44
 Meeting on the Journey   46
 An Ideal Teacher?   50

Inessential and Indispensable   53

Risking Recognition   58

Chapter 3 — On a Shared Communion   63

Guru, Gurus, and the Bala Vidya Mandir   63

Together in God's Hand   67

The *Ultimate* Team Sport   71

Receiving and Showing Promise   75

New Family, New Birth   80

A Shared Communion   85

An Oar Stroke Closer to the Farther Shore   90

Chapter 4 — On the Mystery of Others   93

The Guide   93

An Upset Balance?   96

Stretching the Boundaries of Communion   101

The Beloved Outsider   106

Placing Ourselves in Peter's Shoes   112

A Mystery of Relationship   115

A Different Kind of Harmony?   120

Conclusion — Filling in the Gaps   125

The Big Gap   125

Filling in a Few Gaps   126

Gaps and Limits   130

Spiritual *and* Religious?   132

Getting Started   135

Index of Subjects and Names   136

Index of Scripture References (Hindu and Christian)   140

Acknowledgments

> After he had washed their feet, had put on his robe, and had
> returned to the table, he said to them, "Do you know what I
> have done to you? You call me Teacher and Lord—and you are
> right, for that is what I am. So if I, your Lord and Teacher, have
> washed your feet, you also ought to wash one another's feet. For
> I have set an example, that you also should do as I have done to
> you" (John 13:12-15, NRSV).

In this passage—which I consider one of the most beautiful and
profound texts of the Christian New Testament—Jesus attempts to
shape his disciples into a community of mutual love and service. The
distinguishing mark of those who follow in Jesus' name should, according to his instructions, be their willingness to humble themselves and
wash one another's feet, to love one another as they have been loved
(cf. John 13:34-35). Such a vision of community seems particularly
appropriate now, as I write these acknowledgments. For this present
work, as I see it, is not entirely my own. It is the fruit of much love and
service, freely given by a much broader group of family and friends,
teachers and colleagues, trusted advisors and fellow travelers on the way.

Indeed, although composed in just about four months during the
late summer and early autumn of 2003, *Spiritual but Not Religious?*
actually had several distinct "beginnings"—each with its own distinct
community of love and selfless service. It began, first, as the somewhat
surprising course of my life and spiritual journey, which figures promi-
nently in its pages. Thanks are owed, then, to the many who have
walked ahead and alongside of me on this journey. The sheer breadth of
this great cloud of witnesses prevents me from explicitly acknowledging
many who merit tremendous gratitude and whose influence helped

shape this book, whether they know it or not. For the sake of brevity, I will simply mention my sister Amy; my father Ralph, and stepmother Miriam; my close-knit group of friends and family centered around Athens, Georgia; my outstanding teachers and fellow students at the University of Tennessee at Chattanooga, at the Boston University School of Theology, and at Boston College; Michelle and John Gensheimer, who both—albeit in rather different ways—opened a way for me to the Roman Catholic Church; the academic and residential communities of the Alabama School of Mathematics and Science in Mobile, Alabama; and Dave Shields, S.J., and the volunteers, staff, and students of the Red Cloud Schools in Pine Ridge, South Dakota. Above all, of course, thanks are due to Arlie Herron, Al Humbrecht, Renee Lorraine, and Swami Paramarthananda Saraswati, without whom this book quite literally would not have been possible.

If one "beginning" of this volume was my life journey itself, quite another stemmed from my graduate study and doctoral dissertation, recently completed at Boston College. Relatively little of the prose comes directly from the dissertation, but it is deeply informed by the intensive study of Adi Shankaracharya and Saint Augustine of Hippo that I attempted under the expert guidance of my director Francis X. Clooney, S.J., and my readers Michael J. Himes and Bruce T. Morrill, S.J. Without their support and encouragement, I would never have been bold enough to take on such a complex project. My pursuit of instruction in Shankara and Advaita Vedanta was also facilitated by the warm hospitality of the teachers and staff of Arsha Vidya Gurukulam, in eastern Pennsylvania, as well as the Jesuit communities of Aikiya Alayam and Satya Nilayam/Sacred Heart College in Chennai, India. Much of the dissertation writing itself was completed as a resident scholar at the Institute for Ecumenical and Cultural Research, adjacent to the campus of Saint John's University in central Minnesota. I received a great many helpful suggestions from the institute's executive director Patrick Henry, executive associate Dolores Schuh, C.H.M., liaison officer Wilfred Theisen, O.S.B., and student intern Stephanie Hart, as well as the other 2001–2002 resident scholars: E. Byron Anderson, Charles Bouchard, O.P., Cathy Campbell, Donald Cozzens, Daniel Grigassy, O.F.M., Donald Klinefelter, Sharon McMillan, S.N.D., Mary Margaret Pazdan, O.P., Ernest Ranly, C.P.P.S., and Sharon Reives. It is no accident that the idea of using short autobiographical sketches to illustrate important themes—including the sketches that introduce chapters 1, 2, and 3 of this work—was originally recommended to me by the members of this illustrious group.

The third and final "beginning" of this book was a letter I received from Peter Dwyer, director of Liturgical Press, in early October 2002. At that time he suggested that I consider pulling together a few personal reflections and key insights from my academic work for an entirely different piece of writing intended for a broader audience. Since then I have had the pleasure to work with Linda Maloney, Mark Twomey, Aaron Raverty, O.S.B., and Colleen Stiller at different stages in the proposal, writing, and publication process. To them, and to the many others at Liturgical Press who were instrumental in bringing this work to press, I offer heartfelt thanks. Thanks are also due to the students, staff, and faculty of Saint Joseph College in West Hartford, Connecticut, where I had the tremendous pleasure of teaching while I completed this manuscript. Worthy of particular note are the college chaplain David Cinquegrani, C.P.; my Religious Studies colleagues Ann Marie Caron, R.S.M., and Alex Mikulich; my faculty mentor Mary Alice Wolf; the members of the Humanities and Social Science divisions of the college; and its modest but extraordinary liturgical choir, whose fellowship in song enlivened and sustained my work every week. Though I am sure they did not realize it at the time, Saint Joseph College students Lauren Feldman-Hawley and Maureen Ross Gemme, along with my remarkable landlord and friend Nancy Rubin, gave this book its title and main subject matter by posing exactly the right questions at exactly the right time. For this, I am deeply indebted to them.

A fair range of folks, drawn from many of these different contexts, commented on early drafts of the manuscript, in part or in whole. These readers included Jolie Chrisman, Francis X. Clooney, S.J., Amy Locklin, Buck Marchinton, Deena McKinney, Patricia Weishaar, and Mark Zelinsky. The work was significantly improved by their insights and suggestions.

Finally, I am very grateful to Swami Vagishananda for granting me permission to use modified quotations from his *Vedic Chanting: Self-Study* (Saylorsburg: Arsha Vidya Gurukulam, n.d.) in chapter 3; to the president and manager of Sri Ramakrishna Math in Chennai, India, for permission to use modified quotations from Swami Jagadananda, translator of the *Upadesa Sahasri of Sri Sankaracarya* (Madras: Sri Ramakrishna Math, 1941), throughout the book; and to the musical group Garbage for permission to quote lyrics from their song "Only

Happy When It Rains" in chapter 1. Of course, the rights to these works remain with their original holders.

*   *   *

In the quotation with which I introduced these acknowledgments, Jesus says to his disciples, "You call me Teacher and Lord—and you are right, for that is what I am." Within the Hindu tradition, that great book of law called the *Manusmrti* also speaks about teachers and disciples. In *Manusmrti* 2.144-50, moreover, several comparisons are made between teachers, on the one hand, and mothers and fathers, on the other. The teacher should be regarded as a mother or father, we are told, and the birth bestowed by the teacher is incomparably greater than that bestowed by our natural parents. At the same time, Manu also suggests that the father and mother are actually worth more than a hundred or a hundred-thousand teachers, respectively.

There are various ways that traditional Hindu pundits or historical scholars might reconcile such apparently contradictory statements. When I read them in the context of my own life, however, I simply conclude that sometimes we are privileged to have parents who are also our most profound teachers. And so this book is dedicated to my mother Inge Z. Whittle, who lives in Athens, Georgia, and to my stepfather Egerton Whittle, who passed away almost exactly five years ago. Although they and I never quite saw eye to eye when it came to matters of religion, there is absolutely nothing of value in these pages that I did not, in some important sense, learn first from them.

Reid B. Locklin

Holy Thursday
April 8, 2004
Hartford, Connecticut

Introduction

Raising the Question

The Professor

As a college sophomore in East Tennessee, I certainly would not have called myself Christian. Yet it was at this very time in my life that I wrestled seriously with faith in a God who had assumed human flesh for our salvation. The reason was simple enough: I had enrolled in a course on Indian culture and religion.

The course texts were the twin Hindu epics, *Ramayana* and *Bhagavad-Gita*. In the figure of Rama—hero of the *Ramayana*—I encountered humanity writ large, a dramatic hero journeying, fighting demons, and crossing a great ocean to recover his beloved wife in relentless accord with holy duty, or *dharma*. In the *Gita*, on the other hand, I met the revealer of dharma itself, divinity writ small, the charioteer Krishna. These were the images of an incarnate God with which members of my class were beginning to grapple. Gathered in a circle around the Professor, whose expertise extended from Indian religions through William Faulkner to farming in the Mississippi heartland, we probed these ideals, familiar to some but coming now from an unexpected source. How did these Hindu ideas of incarnation compare with those taught in the Christian Churches?

One of my colleagues, perhaps the most outspoken critic of institutional religion in the class, voiced a strong opinion. "There's nothing special about Christianity. All of these religions are just basically cults of personality." Although I found more value in general notions of God and spiritual life than did my friend, I concurred with his basic point. All religions are the same, for better or for worse. There's nothing that gives a religion like Christianity, or Hinduism for that matter, some kind of privileged status.

The Professor considered the objection for a few moments and smoothed his thin white mustache. "There is something unique," he finally drawled. "Christ."

In retrospect, I know that there are several ways that the Professor might have developed this idea. He might, like the nineteenth-century scholar Adolf von Harnack, have given a long lecture on the unique moral excellence or religious intuition of the historical Jesus of Nazareth, trying to illustrate how this figure stands totally apart, not only from Rama or Krishna, but also from his Jewish and Hellenistic contemporaries. Or the Professor might, like the third- and fourth-century historian Eusebius of Caesarea, have given an account of the remarkable success of the church that followed in this historical figure's wake. Finally, the Professor might, like so many shrill voices in our contemporary world, have insisted upon the uniqueness of Christ and the Church as inviolable principles to which any person of faith must hold absolutely and unrelentingly fast—simply cutting short any voice that ventures to question this assertion.

The Professor, wisely, chose none of these options. Perhaps he saw that they are all, ultimately, dead ends. Instead, he uttered the single word: "Christ." Then he paused, offered a gentle, enigmatic smile . . . and moved on to other topics. In my imagination, the word reverberated throughout the classroom. What makes Christianity unique? Just Christ, that's all: an answer—or, perhaps, non-answer—as obvious as it was elusive. My mind couldn't struggle free of its elegant simplicity.

I was still not yet Christian. But I was intrigued.

Spiritual but Not Religious?

As a convert, theologian and teacher of religious studies some fifteen years later, I invariably find myself in all sorts of conversations about issues of faith and belief. In these conversations, I encounter a wide spectrum of views: liberal, conservative, Christian, Hindu, faithful, skeptical, and sometimes (I fear to admit) downright flaky. But a phrase that seems to arise more and more frequently in these conversations—from all kinds of different people—is one that might once have issued from my own mouth: "I consider myself a very spiritual person, but I am not religious."

It's difficult to know how to respond to this statement. The academic in me wants to parse out and define the relevant terms. "What precisely, Madame or Sir, do you mean by 'spiritual'? What do you mean by 'religious'?" Experience suggests that the first of these two terms can mean almost anything, from some vague New Age ideal discerned in the quotations on a box of herbal tea to a devotion to Christ and Christian dogma as fervent as one could find in any church. The second term typically emerges in much clearer relief: "religious" means some connection or commitment to an *institution*. Whatever spirituality turns out to be, then, it is something to be pursued freely and more or less alone. At best, the authoritarian structures and social constraints of religious institutions serve no useful purpose; at worst, they are positively hurtful and destructive.

Of course, the teacher and plain human being in me could never be satisfied with mere definitions. I want to know the *person,* to ask, "Why? What does this statement reveal about *you*?" From such inquiry emerges a firm conclusion that I might initially resist: namely, that those who make this pronouncement are truly good persons with extremely compelling reasons for refusing to call themselves "religious." They are loyal friends, loving parents, responsible citizens of the nation and of the world, activists for peace, advocates for protecting our natural environment. Not infrequently, they stand apart from the Church or any other religious institution on rather profound grounds of justice or intellectual conviction. The biologist who does not want any part of an organization that could produce even one so-called "scientific creationist." The woman who, struggling most of her life to throw off the belittling sexism she internalized as a child, is understandably reluctant to maintain contact with one of its main perpetrators. The members of a same-sex couple who simply desire to worship and attend public functions without hiding who they are. Finally, the intelligent and sensitive citizen of the world who looks at the diverse religious traditions and ideologies that have defined most people throughout most of history and asks, as did my fellow students fifteen years ago in East Tennessee, "What makes Christianity, or any other religion for that matter, so special?" If the answer is "nothing" or "nothing of any great significance," then the question of institutional commitment hardly arises at all. Or, if it does arise, it does so as an indifferent matter, of little or no consequence to an authentic spiritual life.

There is no disputing the compelling quality of these questions and concerns. At the same time, in the face of the arguments and examples provided by those who would claim to be spiritual without being religious—in whose number are included some of my most valued mentors and closest friends—the Christian convert in me still wonders if the notion makes any sense. It feels like an oxymoron; that is, it feels like a statement that contradicts itself. At least, if it is not an oxymoron, it *should* be. Not only should the terms "spiritual" and "religious" not weigh against each other, but indeed it *should* be unthinkable to claim one without also claiming the other.

Which brings us to this book.

I have already stated that it is hard to know how to respond to the remark, "I consider myself spiritual, but not religious." Yet if there is any reality at all to the claim that Christianity is an inextricably *ecclesial* phenomenon—that is, a faith and tradition that cannot be separated from an *ecclesia,* a church, an institution, or a worshiping assembly— then a response of some kind is absolutely critical. Such a response must attempt to illustrate how authentic spirituality is itself "religious" in the specific sense of opening into commitment to an institution like the Church. We might label such a response "a spirituality of institutional commitment." And so, in brief, this book is intended as a modest contribution to the broader task of implementing such a response and building such a spirituality. Can we really call ourselves spiritual without being religious? Not, I wish to suggest, unless we reduce and attenuate whatever it is we mean by that slippery word "spirituality" itself.

Now, I have deliberately chosen the word "response" rather than "answer" to characterize what I am attempting to do in the pages that follow. It is, of course, possible to give various kinds of answers to those who feel themselves unable or unwilling to commit to an institution like the Church.[1] One could point to Pope John Paul II's remarkably

---

[1] By the word "Church" I intend the one, holy, catholic, and apostolic Church professed by most mainline Christian denominations. The bishops of the Second Vatican Council (1962–65) taught that this true Church of Christ "subsists in" the Roman Catholic Church without being strictly identical to it. See the Dogmatic Constitution on the Church *(Lumen Gentium)* 8, in Austin Flannery, O.P., ed., *Vatican Council II: The Basic Sixteen Documents: Constitutions, Decrees, Declarations: A Completely Revised Translation in Inclusive Language*

humble and candid 1996 pronouncement on evolutionary biology and the origin of the human species.[2] One could offer the example of a congregational church that has opted, as a deliberate act by the whole community, to take an "open and affirming" attitude toward gay women and men. One could draw attention to an international movement like the Order of Saint Benedict, which fostered women as leaders centuries before various secular governments reluctantly permitted them to vote. But such "answers" will never offer more than partial solutions to the most pressing objections. A more credible response will, I think, also end up being more allusive and personal—a soft porch light, left shining to welcome late arrivals inside rather than to demand of them where exactly they have been. So I am attempting a mere "response" rather than a comprehensive "answer." This work is intended as an invitation to consider the question of institutional commitment anew and, at least possibly, from an angle that might not have been imagined or considered before.

This is an ambitious project for such a slim volume. Where to begin? The Fourth Gospel of the Christian New Testament provides a nudge in the right direction.

A Moment of Recognition

> The next day John again was standing with two of his disciples, and as he watched Jesus walk by, he exclaimed, "Look, here is the Lamb of God!" The two disciples heard him say this, and they followed Jesus. When Jesus turned and saw them following, he said to them, "What are you looking for?" They said to him, "Rabbi" (which translated means Teacher), "where are you staying?" He said to them, "Come and see." They came and saw where he was staying, and they remained with him that day. It was about four o'clock in the afternoon (John 1:35-39, NRSV).

When I first decided to use this quotation, I knew what I would write immediately thereafter. I planned to open my commentary with a

(Northport and Dublin: Costello Publishing Company and Dominican Publications, 1996) 9–10.
    [2] See John Paul II, "Message to Pontifical Academy of Sciences on Evolution," *Origins* 26 (December 5, 1996) 414–16.

pithy line: "It begins with a teacher." Once I copied down this text and gave it a moment's thought, however, I realized that such an interpretation would be quite unsuitable. The passage doesn't begin with a teacher; it begins with a moment in time. Specifically, it begins on "the next day" and concludes "at about four o'clock in the afternoon." Compare this to a parallel kind of claim in the Gospel of Luke:

> In the fifteenth year of the reign of Emperor Tiberius, when Pontius Pilate was governor of Judea, and Herod was ruler of Galilee, and his brother Philip ruler of the region of Ituraea and Trachonitis, and Lysanias ruler of Abilene, during the high priesthood of Annas and Caiaphas, the word of God came to John son of Zechariah in the wilderness (Luke 3:1-2).

The author of Luke is all about emperors and rulers and high priests and the mass of details that give the events he describes their rightful place "on the map." The moment at which *he* begins the story is located squarely on the largely secular canvas of world history. The author of the Fourth Gospel shows little interest in such grand persons and events; he simply picks up on the day after the day after the day that John the Baptist bore dramatic witness to an otherwise anonymous face in the crowd (John 1:26)—a face that turns out to belong to Jesus of Nazareth. Now, two days later, John is loitering with two of his disciples, both of whom are also (at least at this point) anonymous.

And what happens? Something as deeply mysterious as it is completely unremarkable. John the Baptist repeats a title that he had given to Jesus the previous day: "the Lamb of God" (v. 36; cf. 1:29). The disciples suddenly identify this relative stranger as worthy of their attention and take a day to see how and where he spends his time. We will learn the results of this otherwise ordinary day only later, when one of these disciples—now named Andrew—seeks out his brother Simon and announces that they have found the Messiah, the Christ, the one anointed by God (1:41). So we are forced to surmise what actually happened. These two anonymous seekers encountered this teacher, saw where he was staying, and were moved by what they saw to make a commitment that would irreversibly transform their own lives and the lives of those countless others who would follow their example from one generation to the next. All this took place, the text reminds us, by about four o'clock in the afternoon.

So it doesn't "begin with a teacher"—at least, not exactly. It begins with that moment when the innermost questions, needs, or desires of the seeker come to rest in a teacher inexplicably well suited to fulfill or transform those very questions, needs, and desires. It could happen on any day and at any hour, even at four o'clock in the afternoon on the day after the day after the day we first stumble across that ideal teacher's path. Yet its consequences will reverberate throughout our lives and, just possibly, the lives of others who follow after us.

The question of institutional commitment is—like religious institutions themselves—tangled, complicated, and often messy. But we have to begin somewhere. I suggest that we begin with seekers, with teachers, and with that crucial moment when their lives are suddenly and unexpectedly bound together. As it turns out, this is an idea that has deep roots both inside and outside the Christian tradition.

Teachers Along the Way

If my brief interpretation of the Fourth Gospel has any merit, it goes some distance toward explaining why this Gospel has proven so attractive to Hindu interpreters.[3] For the process of seeking out the right teacher is a pervasive undercurrent of Hindu life and thought. Consider the following passage from one of the oldest of those scriptural texts called the Upanishads:

> Take, for example, son, a person who is brought here blindfolded from the land of Gandhara and then left in a deserted region. As he was brought blindfolded and left there blindfolded, he would drift about there towards the east, or the north, or the south. Now, if someone were to free him from his blindfold and tell him, "Go that way; the land of Gandhara is in that direction," being a learned and wise person, he would go from village to village asking for directions and finally arrive in the land of Gandhara. In exactly the same way in this world when one has a teacher, he knows: "There is delay for me here only until I am freed; but then I will arrive!"[4]

[3] See, for example, Ravi Ravindra, *Christ the Yogi: A Hindu Reflection on the Gospel of John* (Rochester, Vt.: Inner Traditions, 1998) esp. 24–30.

[4] Chandogya Upanishad 6.14.1-2, in Patrick Olivelle, trans., *Upanisads*, The World's Classics (Oxford and New York: Oxford University Press, 1996) 155 (slightly modified).

The great eighth-century teacher and commentator Adi Shankaracharya looked at this passage and perceived in it an extended metaphor for the individual's spiritual journey from suffering and death to true life, from the bondage of delusion to the freedom of self-knowledge. The seeker encounters an authentic teacher, hears a word of liberation, and "freed from the bandage made of the cloth of ignorance and delusion . . . becomes happy and contented."[5]

Now, it is pretty clear from Shankara's commentary on this passage that he has in mind a deeply traditional image: the disciple who takes refuge with a single teacher and stays with that teacher until the truth has been thoroughly taught by the one and fruitfully assimilated by the other. But close adherence to the literal words of the Upanishad would seem to require at least some attention to those others in the villages who continue to guide the man from Gandhara as he makes his way home. The teacher removes the blindfold and sets the man on his way, to be sure, but after that critical intervention this individual is largely on his own to seek out further instruction and guidance along the way.[6] From the singular "teacher" we arrive, by implication, at the plural "teachers"—all those who direct our steps as we make our way home.

This narrative from the Upanishads serves as a helpful metaphor for my own spiritual journey, a journey that has been inordinately occupied, as it turns out, with complicated, tangled, and sometimes messy questions of institutional commitment. And, from the moment of my initial decision to join the Church to the various steps I have taken to deepen my understanding of this decision, there have been many teachers to direct my steps. Among the vast array of extraordinary individuals whom I might mention, I have singled out a few for special attention in the autobiographical fragments that introduce and frame many of the reflections in these pages. The first of these, the one who first pointed out to me that I was blindfolded and lost, we have already met. I refer to him simply as "the Professor." The others have similarly abstract titles. They are: "the Priest," "the Guru," and "the Guide."

[5] Shankara, Commentary on Chandogya Upanishad 6.14.2, in V. Panoli, trans., *Upanishads in Sankara's Own Words*, vol. 3, rev. ed. (Calicut: Mathrubhumi Printing and Publishing Co., Ltd., 1995) 667.

[6] Naturally Shankara, following the guidance of the scriptural text itself, has an answer to this objection: the journey from village to village functions as a metaphor for the one who, although already possessed of self-knowledge and the liberation it brings, continues to live in this world until the natural death of the body. See ibid., 667–70.

Why titles? Why not use personal names? There are two main reasons why I have decided to employ this somewhat formal and possibly even pretentious device. These reasons do *not* include some kind of misguided attempt to "protect the innocent from discovery." Professor and Priest, Guru and Guide—these are real people, familiar to me and to anyone who knows me well. The first motive for using titles rather than names does, however, follow from a candid recognition that, in articulating my memories of these persons and re-presenting them in writing, I am engaged in as much interpretation as pure reporting. To offer just one example: when I shared the anecdote that introduces chapter 4 with the Guide a few years back, she seemed somewhat taken aback at the way I characterized her sharp criticism of the Church: "You know," she wrote in an email, "I really *like* Catholics." Despite this exchange, I still hang on to the memory in question and feel comfortable retelling it here—it is, indeed, one of the most cherished moments that came out of my baptism, confirmation, and First Communion in the Roman Catholic Church. But I also recognize that I articulate a remembered image of "the Guide" which, although not deliberately fictionalized, has almost certainly grown and developed over the years and is, therefore, not strictly identical with the actual person who made such an impact in the first place. So perhaps some reluctance to identify the remembered Guide with the living person in question is not entirely unreasonable.

The second main reason for using titles rather than names for these companions along the way stems from my purpose in pulling these reflections together in the first place: that is, to offer a response and to extend an invitation. The main thrust of the response will occupy us in chapters 1 and 2, entitled "On Seekers" and "On Teachers," respectively. In these two chapters I attempt to build a portrait of religious institutions somewhat distinct from those with which most of us are familiar, a portrait grounded not upon some abstract principle or hierarchical structure but upon that very moment of recognition we have already encountered in the Fourth Gospel and the Upanishads. From one point of view, religious institutions are revealed and sustained through just such moments of recognition, from one generation to the next—spiritual seekers continually receiving guidance from those teachers they encounter on the way.

The invitation that arises in and through this response will emerge more clearly in chapters 3 and 4: "On a Shared Communion" and

"On the Mystery of Others." In these chapters I endeavor to illustrate how precisely those uncomfortable facts that appear most sharply to challenge the idea of an institutional commitment to the Christian Church—above all, the rather modest and uncertain place of Christianity among the great religions of the world—invite us to view such a commitment as a natural, even indispensable component of the authentic spiritual journey. It may be, as I shall suggest, that we honor the sheer diversity of spiritual paths, not by withholding our trust and withdrawing our commitment, but by entering into them as fully as possible. And this would seem to require participation in one or more religious institutions.

As we shall see, the Professor, Priest, Guru, and Guide will not be our only resources in formulating this response and exploring this invitation. Indeed, the pages of this volume include considerably more exegesis and interpretation than autobiographical reflection. As a scholar and theologian, it would be difficult for me not to draw upon the rich resources of the Hindu and Christian traditions with which I am most familiar—above all, the writings of the Hindu teacher Adi Shankaracharya, whom we have already met, and of the Christian bishop Saint Augustine of Hippo, whom we shall meet shortly. But it is the Professor and Priest, Guru and Guide who will, above all, direct our steps as we make our journey to Gandhara. In drawing on my own personal story in this way, I hope to extend it to the reader, not as a prescriptive norm, but as a general orientation and opportunity to reconsider those whom you have encountered as professors or priests, gurus or guides. Even as I offer what I hope will be a credible spirituality of institutional commitment, I also offer the personal narrative of which this spirituality is the result. I invite you to "try it on," to see whether this gentle porch light is the one welcoming you inside . . . or, if not, whether it might at least provide a little clarity as you pass by on your own journey, wherever it may ultimately lead.

Back to the Beginning

And so we return to the place where we began this introduction. The Professor smoothes his thin white mustache and pronounces the single word: "Christ."

What happens then? Just possibly a moment of recognition, when something crying out silently from the depths of the self hears an answering call from outside. A moment as mysterious as it is completely ordinary. To explore it, we need to look forward and back, to reflect on the process by which we might suddenly or gradually conceive an authentic desire for a truth that will set us free. This is the moment when we emerge as the seekers we were always meant to be.

It is to this moment that we now turn.

Chapter 1

On Seekers

The Priest

Just a few months separated the moment the Professor intrigued me with that single word from the moment I stumbled across the path of the Priest.

It wasn't as though I had never heard the word "Christ" before. In fact, my early years were largely defined by a vague commitment to various Christian communities insofar as they involved me in choir, youth retreats, and comic book treatments of the Apocalypse. Along the way, however, a combination of academic study, a deepening sensitivity to cultural and religious diversity, and a healthy dose of shallow non-conformism had worn down my would-be faith, leaving a more or less secular humanism in its wake. Pressed to give a reason for spurning the Church, I might have used the example of an independent Baptist congregation across the way from the house of a close friend. Internal divisions had driven the congregation to reject one pastor after another; eventually, such divisions led to what I believed was a deliberate torching of the church steeple by an irate parishioner. Much later, I would discover that the steeple had in fact been struck by lightning. But this inconvenient fact did not alter my basic conclusion: as far as I could tell, the only part of the church that appeared to be fulfilling its authentic purpose was the graveyard.

To me, the conclusion from this and other examples of religious dysfunction seemed obvious. The great religions of the world, especially Christianity, resembled the kudzu-draped trees I often saw along highways in my north Georgia home: whatever life-giving idea had once sprouted and reached for the heavens there had long since suffocated under a dark canopy of corrupt institutions and empty religiosity.

As we have already seen, it was the Professor who piqued my curiosity and set me on a new course. Nevertheless, as I began to look at Christianity anew and to test the waters in various faith communities, I renounced none of my criticisms and acted them out in a definite and predictable way. After attending a few services, I would make a private appointment or somehow corner the pastor with a few pointed questions. One of these questions went to the heart of my concerns: "What about corruption in the institutional Church?" The answers I received inevitably struck me as, at best, historically naïve or, at worst, deeply self-deceptive. So I moved from one community to another, searching for a religious leader who could answer my questions with honesty and intelligence, all the while quietly confident that none would.

This is when I encountered the Priest.

We met in his office at the local Catholic student center, where I had attended Mass with friends several times already. The Priest surprised me a bit by coming out from behind his desk and sitting in a chair directly across from me. I was a bit unnerved by his clerical garb and collar, having moved in predominantly Protestant circles thus far, but I suppose I also felt that such obvious institutional accoutrement virtually guaranteed his defeat by the sharp edge of my critique. Besides, by this point I had the pattern down cold. I warmed him up with pleasant banter around my background and studies, asked a few purely informational leading questions about Catholic practice and belief, and then let him have it. "So, what about corruption in the institution? What about all the wrongs that have been committed in the name of the Church?" What, I asserted forcefully in various ways, about the *mess* that you and yours have made of your adherence to this tradition? What about all the failure and injustice? What, in short, about the *real Church* of history and day-to-day life? What about *that*?

I don't remember for sure, but I think the Priest shrugged. "What about it?"

I was stunned into silence. Was this sarcasm or indifference?

Neither, as it turned out. The Priest continued with something like the following. "It's not really the right question, is it? I mean, you're old enough to have seen something of the world. What do you know about organized groups like school administrations, the United States government, or even your clique of closest friends? Whenever people get together to organize much of anything they screw it up. You inevitably find domination, manipulation, and vindictive assaults—rhetorical or actual—on those who are regarded as outsiders. Now apply that insight to what might be the largest single organization in the world. What do you *think* is going to happen?

"So there is massive corruption in the Church. What about it? If you know anything about history or sociology, this is not an interesting question." He leaned forward. "I'll give you a question that *is* interesting. The institutions of the Church are corrupt. Okay. What are you going to do about it? What, *exactly*, is your stake in the question going to be?"

A year and a half later I received baptism, confirmation, and First Communion in the Roman Catholic Church.

I've narrated this story to friends and acquaintances many times. Their reactions almost always involve some degree of surprise or even betrayal. Perhaps they see in the Priest's challenge little more than a clever dodge or subtle form of intimidation; indeed, had the Priest been someone other than who he was, his words *could* well have been merely clever. And clever superficiality is not enough for most of my friends. What *they* expect from me is something on the order of objective inquiry and critical reflection.

In truth, I did engage in a great deal of inquiry and reflection as I formed my intention and prepared for baptism: a summer in biblical study; many weeks musing over distinctively Catholic teachings on Eucharist, a "consistent ethic of life," and the Bishop of Rome; and countless hours of ping-pong, fellowship, and lively conversation with my sponsor. All of these tended to point me toward a reality different from the one I had always taken for granted. The story of the Church, I gradually came to believe, was a story of the surprising work of God *despite* human frailty and institutional corruption. This tree was covered in kudzu, all right, but it was also very much alive. It was alive in and through those bold or honest or fortunate enough to recognize God's grace at work in their lives and to strive, against all legitimate and reasonable expectations to the contrary, to become what the Scriptures declare they already are: a holy and faithful people of God.

Still, this new vision of the Church did not, in and of itself, entirely account for that first moment of challenge and recognition. After years of reflection, I have come to believe that the Priest's critical insight at that first meeting was to see that this story was *already* my own, like it or not. When he asked, "What are you *going* to do about it? What *will be* your stake in the Church?" he revealed that I had already shown myself as a person with something at stake. Otherwise I would never have posed my questions the way that I did. The Priest raised the strangely compelling possibility that this community and its institutions gave a kind of coherence to my journey thus far, including my deep criticisms of this very community and its institutions. The seed was already planted. The Priest had only to point it out and give it room to grow.

Point it out he did. And so, at that moment, in the modest office of a Catholic student center in the mountains of East Tennessee, I discovered—*really* discovered—that my church-hopping was not merely an academic exercise or mind-broadening excursion. At that moment, I suddenly found myself among the ranks of spiritual seekers.

A Moment of Clarity and Disgust

If the American cinema is to be believed, a fairly consistent feature of human experience is the so-called "moment of truth," "moment of clarity," or, more darkly, "moment of reckoning." This is a moment when all those events that have heretofore defined our lives—loves gained or lost, decisions that seemed obvious or inconsequential at the time, actions or failures to act—suddenly appear to have been headed in one direction all along. Everything just falls together. Events conspire to draw us into a new world of possibilities. We step boldly or timidly into this new world . . . or maybe we refuse, retreating back into the old one. Either way, nothing will ever be quite the same.

There is no question in my mind that my initial interview with the Priest might be aptly characterized as a "moment of clarity." After that point, I would always regard my life as something set apart. Nothing ever has been quite the same.

My life might have been set apart, but my experience of personal revelation was not, as such, without precedent or parallel both inside and outside the Christian tradition. In a short work entitled *A Thousand Teachings*,[1] for example, Adi Shankaracharya develops the content and consequences of precisely such a "moment of clarity": that is, a moment when the spiritual seeker realizes that the highest purpose of life is not something that can be achieved through ordinary human effort . . . and thus emerges as an authentic seeker in the truest sense of that term. In the prose portion of this short treatise, our Hindu teacher unfolds a process of self-discovery, wherein such seekers come to view their own true nature and sole reality as ultimately nondifferent from *brahman*, the divine self and foundation of all living beings—eternally free, ever-attained, and therefore beyond all notions of achievement or acquisition.[2] In the accompanying verse portion, he offers further illustrations of this teaching, extols its power to transform the lives of those who make it their own, and refutes opposing views.[3] At the heart of both portions stands a quiet confidence that what is most true, most fulfilling, and most enduring is already a permanent feature of our lives. We are already free, already eternal, already bathed in purifying light. We simply need to open our hearts and minds to see it.

But there is a catch. For Shankara would never have needed to write a treatise like *A Thousand Teachings*, much less his many commentaries and other works, if our hearts and minds simply fell open at the lightest touch. We are more like the recalcitrant lid of a tightly sealed jar: without hot running water, a sharp tap on the floor, or a specially designed "grip" of some kind, we will not budge. In fact, despite all the hot water and tapping in the world, many of us never budge at all. This is so, Shankara suggests, because authentic spiritual pursuit itself depends to a great extent upon a dramatic event that he finds in two scriptural verses from the Upanishads:[4]

[1] Hereafter cited by chapter and verse in its Prose or Verse Portion. Except where otherwise noted, I use the Sanskrit text and English translation in Swami Jagadananda, trans., *Upadesa Sahasri of Sri Sankaracarya* (Madras: Sri Ramakrishna Math, 1941). I have also had frequent reference to Sengaku Mayeda, trans., *A Thousand Teachings: The Upadesasahasri of Sankara* (Albany: State University of New York Press, 1992).

[2] See especially Shankara, *A Thousand Teachings*, Prose Portion 1.25-38 and 2.77-81, 94-97, 110, in Jagadananda, 16–28, 50–52, 58–59, 69–70.

[3] See, for example, Shankara, *A Thousand Teachings*, Verse Portion 12.1-10, 17.25-31 (supporting illustrations), 16.70-73, 17.59-81 (the complete freedom of those who know the self), and 16.23-63, 18.9-25 and passim (refutations), in Jagadananda, 122–25, 189–90, 198–201, 209–15, 220–25ff.

[4] Shankara, *A Thousand Teachings*, Prose Portion 1.3, in Jagadananda, 2–3.

> When he perceives the worlds as built with rites, a Brahmin should acquire a sense of disgust—"What's made can't make what is unmade!"
> To understand it he must go, firewood in hand, to a teacher well-versed in the Vedas and focused on *brahman*.

> To that student of tranquil mind and calm disposition, who had come to him in the right manner, that learned person faithfully imparted,
> The knowledge of *brahman*, by which he understood that [divine] Person—the true, the imperishable.[5]

In a single moment, the seeker sees the world in a new light, relinquishes an old way of life, and takes immediate steps to pursue a new one. Such a decisive realization may take a few seconds or it may take the better part of a lifetime. Without it, however, Shankara implies that the processes of hearing, reflection and meditation prescribed in *A Thousand Teachings* are unlikely to bear their intended fruit.

Now, there is much in the passage that may seem muddy to a reader unfamiliar with Hindu religion and Indian culture. What are "the worlds as built by rites"? Who is a "Brahmin"? What's so great about a tranquil mind, or firewood for that matter? What, in short, are the pieces that make this "moment of clarity" so important for the spiritual seeker? Commenting on these verses in their original literary context, Shankara gathers such issues together under the Sanskrit word *adhikara*.[6] Literally, this term carries a range of possible meanings related to one's rightful "place" or field of action, from diligent effort in one's line of work to the sovereign prerogatives of a king.[7] For Shankara it refers more specifically to one's fitness, qualification, or inherent affinity as a seeker, the culmination of one's journey thus far—including not only this life but countless past lives—and the necessary preparation for the next step.[8] It is what "qualifies" the seeker *as* a true seeker, rather than as something else.

---

[5] Mundaka Upanishad 1.2.12-13, in Olivelle, *Upanisads,* 270–71 (slightly modified).

[6] Shankara, Commentary on Mundaka Upanishad 1.2.12 (introduction), in V. Panoli, trans., *Upanishads in Sankara's Own Words,* vol. 2, rev. ed. (Calicut: Mathrubhumi Printing and Publishing Co. Ltd., 1996) 144.

[7] See Vaman Shivaram Apte, *The Practical Sanskrit-English Dictionary,* rev. ed. (Delhi: Motilal Banarsidas, 1998) 62–63.

[8] See A. G. Krishna Warrier, *The Concept of Mukti in Advaita Vedanta,* Madras University Philosophical Series 9 (Chennai: University of Madras, 1961) 416–23; and Francis X.

Shankara did not invent the word *adhikara*, and his use of the term to elucidate what happens in these verses is almost certainly intended to evoke a cluster of assumptions he would have shared with many of his contemporaries in eighth-century India. These include, most importantly, an assumption that "spirituality" or "spiritual awakening" never takes place in a vacuum, apart from the personal and social conditions of day-to-day existence. If we wish to crack open our old, inherited ways of viewing the world in which we live, we will be helped by a calm heart and a disciplined mind, to which Shankara will elsewhere add humility, compassion, and other "qualities of a disciple."[9] If the spiritual quest is something on which we place great personal value, we will approach it "with firewood in hand," that is, ready for some amount of service and self-sacrifice. If this quest involves study of such Vedic scriptures as the Upanishads, moreover, then it will be pursued by those who, according to the religious and legal prescriptions of Shankara's time and place, have exclusive access to these same scriptures: males drawn from the top three classes of the Hindu caste system.[10] The precise details of this system need not delay us here. What's important for our purposes is simply to note that, when the Upanishad designates this disciple as a "Brahmin," it identifies him as a member of what is traditionally understood as the priestly class of Indian society—the "cream of the crop," in terms of education and social status.

Such social limits in the area of *adhikara* or spiritual qualification may give us pause, and rightly so. In places, Shankara himself will suggest that restrictions on gender and social class are not absolute when it comes to seeking self-knowledge.[11] More frequently, however, he not

---

Clooney, S.J., *Theology after Vedanta: An Experiment in Comparative Theology* (Albany: State University of New York Press, 1993) 129–41.

[9] Shankara, *A Thousand Teachings*, Prose Portion 1.2, in Jagadananda, 2. On the prescribed "qualities of a disciple," see especially Sengaku Mayeda, "Adi-Sankaracarya's Teaching on the Means to Moksa: Jnana and Karman," *Journal of Oriental Research* 34/35 (1966) 72–73; and Anantanand Rambachan, *Accomplishing the Accomplished: The Vedas as a Source of Valid Knowledge in Sankara,* Society for Asian and Comparative Philosophy 10 (Honolulu: University of Hawaii Press, 1991) 85–92.

[10] Clooney, *Theology after Vedanta*, 134–41.

[11] See Arvind Sharma, "Sankara's Life and Works as a Source for a Hermeneutics of Human Rights," in *New Perspectives on Advaita Vedanta: Essays in Commemoration of Professor Richard DeSmet, S.J.*, ed. Bradley J. Malkovsky, Numen Book Series 85 (Leiden: Brill, 2000) 109–21. Cf. Sengaku Mayeda, "Sankara and Narayana Guru," in *Interpreting across Boundaries: New Essays in Comparative Philosophy*, ed. Gerald James Larson and Eliot Deutsch (Princeton, N.J.: Princeton University Press, 1988) 184–202.

only accepts such restrictions but intensifies them, so that they acquire entirely new significance. For example, Shankara suggests that members of the Brahmin caste alone are "particularly fit" as seekers not arbitrarily, but specifically, because he judges that they alone possess a kind of natural affinity for interior detachment and renunciation, preferably as wandering monks.[12] So prominent and so forceful is the mutual association Shankara builds between such inherent affinity for renunciation and the Brahmin class that at least one contemporary Hindu Swami has suggested that they can be regarded as virtual synonyms. Shankara himself seems to have insisted that only Brahmins, along with other upper-caste males, are specially qualified for spiritual instruction; but it is also possible to argue that only those who are qualified for spiritual instruction can really be counted as Brahmins. That is, "Brahmin" becomes a kind of shorthand for any person, of any gender or social class, who arrives at a "moment of clarity" like that depicted in the Upanishad.[13]

Which turns us back to the moment itself. What is it, exactly, that takes place in this narrative? A prospective seeker gives close, critical attention to the "worlds as built by rites," glossed by Shankara as the universe envisioned by the Vedic scriptures themselves: a world of heavens and hells, a world of religious institutions and regulations, and above all a world characterized by the performance or nonperformance of sacred ritual.[14] We might call it the world of conventional religion:

---

[12] Shankara, Commentary on Mundaka Upanishad 1.2.12, in Panoli, vol. 2, 145–46. For more extended discussions of the connection between self-knowledge and formal renunciation as a wandering mendicant, see Clooney, *Theology after Vedanta*, 141–49; Roger Marcaurelle, *Freedom through Inner Renunciation: Sankara's Philosophy in a New Light* (Albany: State University of New York Press, 2000) esp. 131–61; Patrick Olivelle, *Renunciation in Hinduism: A Medieval Debate: Volume One: The Debate and the Advaita Argument* (Vienna: Institut für Indologie der Universität Wien, 1986); Karl H. Potter, "Samkaracarya: The Myth and the Man," in *Charisma and Sacred Biography*, ed. Michael A. Williams, *Journal of the American Academy of Religion Studies* 48/3-4 (1982) 115–19.

[13] See especially Swami Dayananda, *Introduction to Vedanta: Understanding the Fundamental Problem*, ed. Barbara Thornton (New Delhi, Bombay, and Hyderabad: Vision Books, 1989, 1997) 24–27. As one might expect, Swami Dayananda's interpretation stretches Shankara's explicit statements on the issue. Socially conservative commentators translate "Brahmin" more literally as referring *both* to the social class *and* to the sense of renunciation that goes with it. See, for example, P. Sankaranarayanan, trans., *Vivekacudamani of Sri Sankara Bhagavatpada, with an English Translation of the Commentary in Samskrt by Jagadguru Sri Candrasekhara Bharati Svaminah* (Bombay: Bharatiya Vidya Bhavan, 1988) 3–12.

[14] Shankara, Commentary on Mundaka Upanishad 1.2.12, in Panoli, vol. 2, 145.

going to Church or Temple, performing the prescribed prayers and rituals, expecting to be rewarded for faithfulness or punished for disobedience. In response to this view of things, which would presumably have shaped this Brahmin's life thus far, a personal revelation bubbles dramatically to the surface: "what's made can't make what is unmade!" The words may seem a bit cryptic, but the disposition behind them emerges in pretty clear relief. Indeed, the fitness of the seeker can, from one point of view, be reduced to a single expression from the Upanishad.

In Sanskrit, the expression is *nirveda,* rendered above as "a sense of disgust." And it is upon precisely such disgust that everything else will depend.

Beautiful Garbage

Criticism of the institutional Church. A sense of disgust for "the worlds as built by rites." At first glance, these do not offer a promising foundation for what I am calling, for lack of a better term, a spirituality of institutional commitment. And it's true: if criticism and disgust stand alone at the end of the spiritual journey, then there really is no room for institutional commitment or, perhaps, for any commitment at all. But disgust may not be a final word in this matter. Perhaps the seeker does acquire *nirveda* in the face of conventional religion and ritual performance, and perhaps this "sense of disgust" does become an absolutely essential step in the authentic spiritual journey. If so, Shankara suggests, the disgust that comes to light will be of a very specific type.

This disgust will be born of desire.

One day, midway through my first undergraduate course as a teaching fellow, I literally stalked into the classroom and wrote the radio call numbers for some local hip-hop and alternative music stations on the board. "To understand the *Bhagavad-Gita,*" I announced, "you need to confront death and desire. Since most pop music inevitably files down the sharp edges of desire and diminishes the hard facts of death, I suggest that you listen to one of *these* stations before you sit down to read. I think it will help."

I rather doubt that even one member of the class followed my advice, but the pronouncement generated a ripple of shock and amusement.

Some students almost certainly viewed it as a doomed attempt on my part to convince them that I am "hip" or "with it." It wasn't, and I'm not. I know very little about contemporary music other than a smattering of artists and songs I happen to like. What I *am*, however, is thoroughly convinced that hip-hop and "alternative" music helps me to become a better reader of ancient Hindu texts.

One musical group that, at least to my way of thinking, clearly supports this conviction is "Garbage," that brilliant combination of Scottish vocalist Shirley Manson with three instrumentalists based in Madison, Wisconsin. I first encountered the music of Garbage when working as a hall director and mathematics teacher at a residential high school in southern Alabama, and it gained special significance for me later, at a time when the unforeseen fallout of desire and repression of desire briefly reduced my personal life to utter chaos. My interest in the group has persisted, however, due in no small part to the clarity and irony of their music, a clarity and irony revealed especially well in the lyrics of one of their most popular songs:

> I'm only happy when it rains.
> I'm only happy when it's complicated.
> And though I know you can't appreciate it.
> I'm only happy when it rains.
>
> You know I love it when the news is bad,
> And why it feels so good to feel so sad.
> I'm only happy when it rains.[15]

Garbage not only depicts the inevitable results of a culture obsessed with romantic love and sexual fulfillment—emotional domination, revenge fantasies, crippling breakups that require heavy medication—but they portray such results as desirable in and of themselves. I have on occasion, and only somewhat playfully, referred to their artistic corpus as "a musical celebration of codependency."

How does this connect to Hindu texts? Well, although their final conclusions would seem to differ rather profoundly, Shankara's Brahmin disciple and the music of Garbage share a certain uncompromising view of human desire, one that refuses to file it down or dress it up as

---

[15] Garbage, "Only Happy When It Rains," *Garbage*, AMSD 800004, Almo Sounds, Inc., 1995.

something that it is not. Consider the title of Garbage's third album, released in 2001: *beautifulgarbage*.[16] To call what is beautiful "garbage" or, conversely, to call what is garbage "beautiful"—both suggest a radical reorientation of who we are and what we value. When I think of this, I am reminded of a visualization practice I once encountered in a class on Indian Buddhism.[17] Imagine someone you consider beautiful, a supermodel perhaps, or maybe a parent or close friend. Spend some time considering the ways in which this person is beautiful: flawless teeth or skin, a glowing or deeply caring personality, a "cut" or shapely figure, whatever it is that makes that person an object of desire.

Now imagine the same person again, this time from the inside out: a mass of bone and blood and bowels. Still beautiful, still an object of desire? Perhaps, but very likely "beauty" has come to mean something different than it did before. For most of us, the beauty of the intestinal tract resides mainly in the life it helps sustain, in the living person who could not exist without it. Its beauty is found in something more, albeit a "something more" inseparable from the intestines themselves.

I would pair this visualization strategy with the more concrete and practical exercise of examining the contents of a garbage can. What's in there? My own brief foray beneath the kitchen sink reveals coffee grounds, dust and loose hair swept up from the floor, a burned-out headlight, some food packaging, several cantaloupe rinds, and the like. Very few of these items never had any value at all. Some have broken or become worn out; most have simply fulfilled their intended purpose. Walking through the grocery store, for example, it was the rinds that attracted me to the cantaloupes in the first place, for that was the only part of the fruit I could see. But the largely futile tapping, weighing, and smelling I used to decide which one to buy revealed an important aspect of the disposition I brought to them. The beauty of these rinds is found in something more, albeit a "something more" that they themselves contain. Cantaloupe rinds turn our desires inside out, transforming them and directing them to the fruit that lies inside the initial object of these same desires.

Perhaps this analogy gives us a point of entry to reconsider the profound "sense of disgust" that motivates spiritual pursuit. According to

---

[16] Garbage, *beautifulgarbage*, compact disk 0694931152, Interscope Records, 2001.

[17] Cf. "The Foundations of Mindfulness," in Walpola Rahula, *What the Buddha Taught*, 2nd ed. (New York: Grove Wedenfeld, 1974) esp. 110–13.

Shankara's interpretation, those seekers who conceive a true desire for "what is unmade"—for *brahman,* for God, for the divine Person at the root of all beings, for that imperishable truth which cannot be acquired or achieved by means of "what's made"—these seekers do not merely exchange one set of desires for another. Desire *itself* is turned inside out, irreversibly transformed by the very object it seeks. The problem with "the worlds as built by rites" does not reside in the rites or in any of the other actions that govern human life, as such. Nor is there a problem with human desire, as such. A problem emerges only if and as the daily pursuits of ordinary life, religious observance or any other legitimate field of action are invested with an ultimate significance for which they are entirely unsuited. To seek unlimited, spiritual fulfillment from any or even all such limited actions and experiences is to wrest from them a promise they can never keep, in and of themselves. It's just not their nature. They are the cantaloupe rind, not the fruit; they catch our eye only to point within and beyond themselves.

When regarded as objects of beauty and desire in and of themselves, then, the various pursuits that define our lives, including even the pursuit of conventional religion as generally understood, will eventually emerge as useless garbage, worthy only of disgust. When regarded precisely as garbage, as objects whose ultimate beauty is found in something greater than themselves, on the other hand, they can be seen to embody or contain this very beauty itself.

Split Down the Middle by Hope and Desire

For Christians, there is perhaps no better symbol of beautiful garbage than Jesus of Nazareth, whose true beauty resided exclusively in a "something more" inseparable from his own humanity. Consider the following passage from the Gospel of Mark:

> Jesus went on with his disciples to the villages of Caesarea Philippi; and on the way he asked his disciples, "Who do people say that I am?" And they answered him, "John the Baptist; and others, Elijah; and still others, one of the prophets." He asked them, "But who do you say that I am?" Peter answered him, "You are the Messiah." And he sternly ordered them not to tell anyone about him.

> Then he began to teach them that the Son of Man must undergo great suffering, and be rejected by the elders, the chief priests, and the scribes, and be killed, and after three days rise again. He said all this quite openly. And Peter took him aside and began to rebuke him. But turning and looking at his disciples, he rebuked Peter and said, "Get behind me, Satan! For you are setting your mind not on divine things but on human things" (Mark 8:27-33).

Many biblical scholars and theologians read this passage as the beginning of what has come to be known as "christology." It raises our view from the teaching and healing ministry of an extraordinary human being to this same human being's unique and decisive identity as the Messiah, the Christ, the one anointed by God for a great work of salvation. It also sets the stage for what most Christians regard as the premiere work of this ministry and highest revelation of this identity: his suffering, death, and resurrection.

All of this is quite correct. At the same time, I am slowly becoming convinced that the passage is not really about Jesus of Nazareth at all. It's about Peter, about one of the disciples who has attached himself to this great teacher and healer, about *his* desires and *his* expectations. The question posed by Jesus, after all, is not "Who am I?" but "Who do *you* say that I am?" When Peter speaks, he does not so much offer a firm, reasoned conclusion as give expression to a hope he has been cradling quietly in his heart for some time. We can almost feel a palpable release of tension, a sigh of relief as the words escape his mouth. There, he has finally said it. Now how will Jesus respond?

We know from the passage that Jesus responds in two rather different ways. The first is a request for secrecy. The second is a harsh rebuke.

The stark simplicity of this twofold response, moreover, sets Mark's retelling of the event apart from parallel accounts elsewhere in the Gospels. The Gospel of Luke omits the rebuke altogether: Jesus simply accepts Peter's words, swears the disciples to secrecy and offers a prediction of his suffering, death, and resurrection (Luke 9:18-22). The Gospel of Matthew preserves the rebuke, but adds something to the request for secrecy: an extended passage in which Jesus praises Peter as blessed by God, the foundation of the Church and keeper of the "keys of heaven" (Matt 16:17-19). Each alternate retelling in its own way deflects our attention from the very human figure of Peter and his very human desires. In Mark, Peter is neither protected from rebuke nor praised for what he has to say. He is depicted instead as an ordinary person in a state of internal conflict, split down the middle by hope and desire.

Hope and desire for what? Most Christian preachers, in my experience, will tell us that Peter's confession of Jesus as "Messiah" or "Christ" likely reflects Jewish expectations of a warrior figure who would lead the nation of Israel in victory against its Roman oppressors. Yet any sustained study of first-century Israel suggests that this is just one of a number of possibilities. The very diversity of responses to the question "Who do people say that I am?" hints at what we now know was a wide diversity of beliefs and expectations among first-century Jews. So we can't say for sure what *exactly* "Messiah" might have meant to Peter when he uttered the word. We know that, at least in this passage, it's not a title Jesus chooses for himself; he prefers "Son of Man." We also know that Jesus does not want his identity as Messiah to get around. Possibly he fears it will be misunderstood, or maybe he just wants to avoid the publicity. Whatever the reason, his swearing of the disciples to secrecy renders the whole event more intimate and personal. Peter's confession of his master as Messiah, along with all the hopes, dreams, and expectations revealed in this moment of profound vulnerability, binds the disciples together and sets them apart.

But not, it seems, far enough apart. Whatever hopes, dreams, and expectations Peter places in Jesus, they do not include suffering and death. It is tempting to read Jesus' rebuke—"you are setting your mind not on divine things but on human things"—together with the words pronounced in disgust by Shankara's prospective disciple—"What's made can't make what is unmade." Peter has mistaken the rind for the fruit, has placed his hopes upon this extraordinary human being as he appears to be, rather than as he truly is and will be revealed. This seeker has not yet allowed his genuine and otherwise legitimate desire for security, for freedom, for whatever it is he means by that word "Messiah," to be turned inside out and thoroughly transformed. His hopes and expectations themselves have to undergo a kind of death and resurrection no less profound than that which the Messiah will endure.

Peter has taken a risk, to be sure, but he has not risked enough. He has not, perhaps, risked his own expectations about how exactly these things *should* work themselves out. He has not risked himself.

A Care Package from the Lord

Perhaps Peter's reluctance reveals its own kind of insight. For, if the problem with desires resides exclusively in our tendency to invest whatever objects we desire with a permanence or fulfillment they themselves cannot provide, this emerges most clearly at the other end of the equation, where ordinary and legitimate desires appear to fall barren or wither away, once and for all. This Peter sees clearly, but his refusal to let it transform his most cherished hopes and expectations earns him a harsh rebuke. Still, I sympathize with Peter. In part, I sympathize because I very recently received a similar kind of rebuke all my own.

Early in the summer, when I was just beginning to put this manuscript into writing, I received a card in the mail. It informed me of a certified package at the local post office, awaiting my signature for its release. I couldn't quite make out what was handwritten in the tiny "sender" box, but it seemed to be "Lord."

Surely I was misreading the card. Yet the very idea fascinated and delighted me. A care package from the Lord? Just what I need! I drove down to the post, smiling to myself the whole way. I cheerfully waited in line. When the time came, I gave the clerk my signature, and he handed over the package. It was small and heavy, neatly wrapped in brown paper, sporting a large white label with a return address. And, as it turned out, the sender was indeed "Lord": Lord and Taylor, a funeral home in Athens, Georgia.

That's when it hit me. The box contained the cremains of my stepfather Egerton, who had died suddenly and unexpectedly a little over four years before.

It would be impossible to recount all of the images that tumbled through my mind, one over another, as I sat in the car outside the post office, palms sweaty against the steering wheel and that awful box sitting like a squat gravestone in the passenger seat. I think the first memory that occurred to me was one of the most vivid from that worst day in my life thus far: sitting at the desk in my Boston apartment, picking up the telephone with a slightly trembling hand, hearing one of my dearest friend's equally trembling voice on the other end.

"How are you doing?"

"Better than some."

"You got my email, then."

Long pause. "What email?"

"Oh, how did you hear, then?"

The conversation continued. But slowly, chillingly, my friend and I realized the unthinkable: we were referring to completely different tragedies. One was Edge, the most consistent and caring paternal presence of my teens and early adulthood, at that moment unconscious in an Athens area hospital after two cardiac arrests the night before, victim of a staph infection contracted in the course of treatment for an unrelated condition. The other was Jennifer, a high school classmate and significant maternal presence for my adopted family of intimate friends, at that moment comatose in a Las Vegas hospital, victim of a pancreatic disorder no one had remotely foreseen even one short week before. By the time my plane touched down on Georgia soil the evening of April 17, 1999, both lay dead. Funeral plans were already underway.

"I honestly don't know what to wish for." These words, spoken to my friend during that terrible phone call, have remained true each and every day since. For me, the sudden and pointless deaths of Edge and Jennifer—along with the sudden and pointless suffering brought to my mother and sister, to Jennifer's husband, son, parents, and siblings, and to many others deeply affected by their loss, including me—raises a sharp challenge to wishing for anything at all. I *wish* my mother and I had chosen different doctors, a different hospital, a different course of treatment, anything that might have protected Edge from the bacteria that killed him. I *wish* someone had known the unknowable about Jennifer's pancreas and taken appropriate steps to keep her alive.

Mainly, of course, I just wish Jennifer and Edge *were* still alive. This seems a fairly normal human desire, and it was reflected back to me in two dreams from the year following their deaths.

In the first, my group of friends from high school met Jennifer at a local Dairy Queen. We ordered, and then we walked outside with our food to enjoy the warm sun and each other on a lazy summer afternoon. In the second dream, I found myself walking into a bedroom I did not recognize, with a proof copy of my first academic article in hand. My stepfather was sitting there on the edge of the bed just as he used to sit on the living room sofa every morning, not yet dressed for work and sipping coffee from an insulated mug. I sat down beside him, showed him the article proofs and said, "I wish you could have seen this. You would have been proud." Edge put his hand on my arm. "I *do* see it, and I *am* proud."

I still feel shaken and touched when I remember these dreams, years later. Yet I also recognize that both fall neatly into what that great father of psychotherapy, Sigmund Freud, doubtless would have called "wish-fulfillment," my subconscious giving expression to those desires I have trouble admitting to myself when I am awake. But that opens an important question, a question that Freud himself asked of the spiritual quest in its entirety: is that *all* it is? Is it *merely* fulfillment of a sub-conscious desire? The answer, it seems to me, has to be both yes and no. Certain excruciating details in both dreams offered clues that the de-sires they were enacting would never be fulfilled, at least—and this is absolutely critical—not in any way I could so easily imagine. When Edge laid his hand on my arm, the hand itself was ice cold, the hand of a corpse rather than of a living person. In the other dream, sitting at a small picnic table just outside the Dairy Queen, Jennifer was as ani-mated and cheerful as my happiest memories of her. Yet the rest of us were restless and uncomfortable. Finally, I caught the gaze of another close friend at the table, and it suddenly became all too clear what was happening: every one of us, save Jennifer herself, knew that she was dead. It weighed heavily that not one of us had the heart to tell her.

I woke from the dream as from a nightmare. And it *was* a kind of nightmare, the nightmare of getting exactly what you wish for. "What's made can't make what is unmade," even in our imagination. Our dreams and wishes are bound to fall short—this is certain. But I do not think this necessarily means that they have nothing to tell us about what is ultimately real, beautiful and true. Indeed, the very fact that our dreams and wishes fall short suggests to me, not that they are empty, but that they point beyond themselves to their own death and resurrec-tion, forward or backward toward a deeper truth that just might leave us simultaneously shattered and transformed.

I firmly believe that the bond joining me to Egerton and Jennifer was not severed by their sudden and pointless deaths, but I know with-out a doubt that every word, image, or idea I use to describe this bond will somehow fail. I am left silent and aching.

And so I did in fact sit for a few minutes in silence on that early summer day, hands on the steering wheel, box of cremains in the pas-senger seat of my car—that terrible care package from the Lord. A little over a week later, my mother and I would carry those ashes into upstate New York and scatter them at the graveside of Edge's own mother, in the town he loved more than any other place on this earth. It was not a proper end, by any means—and what could be? Nevertheless, it seemed the proper thing to do.

And where does it leave us, here and now? It leaves us scattering ashes at the edges of gravesides, reflecting upon the rinds of our existence—the exquisitely beautiful garbage on which our lives are hung. In a sense our lives themselves *are* the beautiful garbage. They call us within and beyond our very selves. They call us to conversion.

Gifts of Conversion

At this point, we may seem to have traveled rather far afield from where our journey in *these* pages began. Hopefully this is not actually the case. The Brahmin who conceives a sense of disgust for "the worlds as built by rites"; the disciple Peter, torn in half by hope and desire; even my own subconscious, bringing home with brutal clarity the beauty and futility of whatever it is I *think* I wish for in the face of pointless suffering and death—all of these are images of conversion, albeit images of a conversion that may precede, follow, or even have no connection at all with any rite of initiation or profession of faith. It is the conversion we experience if and when we recognize a yearning for fulfillment beyond anything our otherwise legitimate expectations and desires can ever, in and of themselves, hope to reach.

But how exactly does such conversion take place? What precipitates it, and where does it lead? Perhaps no great work of Western literature asks these questions more forcefully than the *Confessions* of that fourth- and fifth-century convert and "Doctor of the Church," Saint Augustine of Hippo. Books 1–3 portray a young North African rhetorician who thoroughly rejects the Catholic Church of his upbringing on the basis of the crudity and barbarity of its Holy Scriptures.[18] Books 11–13 give an indirect portrait of a considerably older man, a bishop of Hippo and influential leader in that very North African Church he once rejected,

---

[18] See especially Augustine of Hippo, *Confessions* 3.5.9–10.18, in Henry Chadwick, trans., *Augustine: Confessions,* The World's Classics (Oxford and New York: Oxford University Press, 1991) 40–49. Also worthwhile are the beautiful accounts of Augustine's early life in Peter Brown, *Augustine of Hippo* (Berkeley and Los Angeles: University of California Press, 1967) 28–45, and Garry Wills, *Saint Augustine,* Penguin Lives (New York: Viking Penguin, 1999) 1–30.

himself offering a penetrating reading of those same Scriptures he once thought crude and barbaric.[19] Quite a transformation.

Joining the young erudite to the Christian bishop is an extraordinary spiritual journey, narrated especially in books 4–9. This journey ranges to such places as Rome and Milan, through the pseudo-Christian Manichee sect and the philosophy of such great minds as Cicero and Plotinus, into Augustine's complex relationship with his mother, and to the accompaniment of much weeping. It reveals a growing apprehension of God and deepening appreciation for the spiritual life. Yet beneath this account lies a quiet conviction that what is being described in such rich detail merely fleshes out a "moment of clarity" no less definitive than that of Shankara's Brahmin disciple, a moment driven by its own kind of burning desire and profound disgust. For Augustine in particular, the spiritual quest is driven by a deeply embedded desire for the life we might imagine for ourselves: a life of consistently sound judgments, genuinely unselfish love, and lasting contentment. And this desire in turn generates disgust for that "other law" described in the Christian Scriptures (e.g., Rom 7:21-25), a pernicious and pervasive force that seems always to weaken our judgment, to taint our love, and to keep us looking over our shoulder in resentment at the apparent happiness of others.[20] Whether we choose to call this weakness a "law" or not, we walk a landscape cluttered with its debris: systemic poverty and injustice, failed or hollow relationships, those kind words we neglect to offer, that sharp retort we later regret.

In Augustine's own case, the power exerted by this "other law" comes to clear expression in a telling phrase from his adolescence: "Grant me chastity and continence, but not yet."[21] By his early thirties, as an orator in the imperial court of Milan, he had satisfied many of his intellectual objections to the Church and its Scriptures.[22] Through

---

[19] Cf. Brown, *Augustine of Hippo*, 177–81.

[20] Cf. Augustine of Hippo, *Propositions from the Epistle to the Romans* 45–46, in Paula Fredriksen Landes, trans., *Augustine on Romans: Propositions from the Epistle to the Romans; Unfinished Commentary on the Epistle to the Romans* (Chico: Scholars Press, 1982) 16–19, and the somewhat later *To Simplician on Various Questions* 1.1.12-15 in J.H.D. Burleigh, trans., *Augustine: Earlier Writings* (Philadelphia: Westminster Press, 1953) 381–83.

[21] Augustine of Hippo, *Confessions* 8.7.17, in Chadwick, 145.

[22] This is a prominent theme of chapters 6 and 7 of the *Confessions*. See also Brown, *Augustine of Hippo*, esp. 79–100.

friends and mentors, he had also heard a virtual *Who's Who* of prominent conversion stories—each of them irreducibly unique, but each leading inexorably to the Church.[23] Neither his intellectual conviction nor these persuasive stories, however, offered sufficient incentive for Augustine to leave behind his moderately self-indulgent style of life, love, and career ambition. He wanted to move beyond these desires and pursuits, but he found himself unable to do so. His whole life called out for thorough conversion.

Perhaps the most remarkable features of Augustine's tale are the details of his conversion itself, when it finally comes to him. If neither intellectual acumen nor good company, in and of themselves, could empower this would-be spiritual seeker to leave behind old habits and desires in the pursuit of a new way of life, whatever could? As it turns out, this more daunting task is accomplished by a couple of otherwise insignificant events in a Milan garden: an unidentified child's voice repeating the phrase *tollo lege*, "pick up and read"; an unremarkable passage from the apostle Paul enjoining its readers to eschew lives of revelry in favor of a life in Christ (Rom 13:13-14), itself picked at random in response to that child's mysterious call.[24] "At once, with the last words of this sentence," Augustine writes in the *Confessions*, "it was as if a light of relief from all anxiety flooded into my heart."[25] Shortly after this event, he submitted his name to the bishop of Milan for baptism in the Church.[26]

Now, it can hardly be doubted that Augustine uses this rather idiosyncratic story to illustrate an insight he had earlier gained from an intensive study of the Pauline epistles in the New Testament.[27] Conversion, Augustine concluded from his careful reading of these letters, is

---

[23] Augustine of Hippo, *Confessions* 8.2.3–7.16 in Chadwick, 133–45.

[24] Ibid., 8.12.29, in Chadwick, 152–53.

[25] Ibid., in Chadwick, 153.

[26] Ibid., 9.5.13, in Chadwick, 163.

[27] On the decisive influence of Augustine's Pauline commentaries on both the *Confessions* and his entire subsequent development, see especially William S. Babcock, "Augustine's Interpretation of Romans (A.D. 394–396)," *Augustinian Studies* 10 (1979) 55–74; F. Edward Cranz, "The Development of Augustine's Ideas on Society before the Donatist Controversy," *Harvard Theological Review* 14 (1954) 277–300; Paula Fredriksen, "Beyond the Body/Soul Dichotomy: Augustine on Paul Against the Manichees and the Pelagians," *Recherches Augustiniennes* 23 (1988) 89–105; Paula Fredriksen, "*Excaecati Occulta Justitia Dei*: Augustine on Jews and Judaism," *Journal of Early Christian Studies* 3 (1995) 306–13; and Eugene TeSelle, *Augustine the Theologian* (New York: Herder and Herder, 1970) 156–65.

not really a "decision," at least not in the usual sense of that term. It is more like a gift. When Augustine finally ends his cycle of procrastination and makes a commitment to Christ and the Church, for example, this emerges less from stern self-discipline than from a profound transformation of his desires themselves: "Suddenly it had become sweet to me to be without the sweets of folly. What I once feared to lose was now a delight to dismiss."[28] The gift-quality of such transformation is further underscored by how it reaches its recipient in such a personal, intimate way. Augustine treated the child's voice and scriptural verses as a direct communication from God. Nevertheless, when he shared the all-important biblical quotation with his friend Alypius, who had accompanied him into the garden, Alypius' gaze instantly skipped down the page to a completely different verse. Why? Augustine alludes to a possible explanation: since Alypius had always maintained higher moral standards than Augustine, Paul's admonition to leave behind a dissolute life was not what he needed to hear.[29] Although the two friends would receive baptism together, they had, as different persons with different life experiences and different pressing issues of concern, received different gifts of conversion.

In a letter to one of his mentors, written a few years before the *Confessions,* Augustine captures the unique character of conversion as a personal, intimate gift with the Latin adverb *congruenter.*[30] Confronted, on the one hand, with scriptural texts that declare the reception of grace a gift of God rather than a result of human effort and, on the other, with innumerable biblical examples of widely diverging reactions to the same events in Jesus' ministry, Augustine concludes that God chooses to call some persons *congruenter,* usually translated "effectually," but more literally rendered "fittingly" or "conformably." That is, for those destined to receive salvation, God does not simply issue a blanket invitation; on the contrary, the grace of conversion comes to them in a way that conforms to their irreducibly unique histories and personalities and thus enables them to respond in freedom and delight.[31] There is no "one size

[28] Augustine of Hippo, *Confessions* 9.1.1, in Chadwick, 155. See also Margaret R. Miles, *Desire and Delight: A New Reading of Augustine's Confessions* (New York: Crossroad Press, 1991) esp. 3–35, 42–43.

[29] Augustine of Hippo, *Confessions* 8.12.30, in Chadwick, 153.

[30] See especially Augustine of Hippo, *To Simplician on Various Questions* 1.2.13-14, in Burleigh, 395–96.

[31] Augustine of Hippo, *To Simplician on Various Questions* 1.2.21, in Burleigh, 404–5. Also see Brown, *Augustine of Hippo,* esp. 154–56.

fits all" in the transformation of will and desire that characterize the authentic spiritual seeker.

Not surprisingly, this portrait of conversion has excited a great deal of controversy from Augustine's time to our own, particularly insofar as it entirely eclipses human free will in matters of salvation.[32] Regardless, we can still see in Augustine's theology and rich account of his own conversion an assumption we also discovered in the teaching of Adi Shankaracharya: namely, the assumption that "spirituality" or "spiritual awakening" never takes place in a vacuum, apart from the personal and social conditions of day-to-day existence. For Shankara, this means that, at least ordinarily, only certain types of persons from certain types of background possess *adhikara* or fitness for spiritual pursuit; for Augustine, it means that each and every one of that improbably diverse group of persons drawn to the name of Christ must have been called *congruenter*, in ways suited to their diverse backgrounds, personal histories and innermost motivations. Either way, as seekers, we are never called as other than who we are, here and now. We may indeed be seeking a truth beyond what we can reasonably hope, imagine or desire, but this truth comes to us by means of those very hopes, imaginings, and desires themselves.

Does this mean that we are not called to change? Well, Augustine decides to leave behind his old life and take up a new one. So, in his own way, does Shankara's Brahmin disciple. Perhaps it would be least inaccurate to say that spiritual seekers inevitably make a change when we seek to become who we really, behind all the masks we have created or had placed upon us, already are. And, for precisely this reason, there is no way around our most cherished hopes and desires. The only way is through them.

Who We Are

So, now we can ask a question that has been hovering on the edges of this entire chapter: who exactly are these people we call "spiritual seekers"?

---

[32] See Fredriksen, "Beyond the Body/Soul Dichotomy," 94–98; John M. Rist, "Augustine on Free Will and Predestination," *Journal of Theological Studies N.S.* 20 (1969) 420–49; and TeSelle, 176–82.

In a short treatise entitled *On Instructing the Uninstructed*—a work that resembles Shankara's *A Thousand Teachings* in many ways—Augustine discusses the various reasons people give for seeking out spiritual instruction and baptism in the Church.[33] There are those seekers who have received some "warning or dread inspired from on high," possibly by means of dreams or miracles.[34] There are others who have instead "been moved to that decision by books, whether the canonical Scriptures or those of good writers."[35] Still others are not spiritual seekers at all: they seek out instruction strictly in order to advance their social standing. But even these, he insists, should not be turned away. They may yet become what they are now pretending to be.[36]

To this short list of prospective seekers we might add others. Shankara's disciple, who examines the social and religious world that surrounds him and exclaims, "What's made can't make what is unmade!" Peter, who finally pronounces his deepest hopes and expectations by calling his master by that multilayered and ambivalent title, "Messiah." Augustine himself, moved by a child's voice and a random verse of Scripture to abandon a conventional life of romantic love and career success. And to this more illustrious group I have been bold to include myself as well, sitting behind the steering wheel of my car and also—some fifteen years earlier—facing the Priest in a modest office at a Catholic student center in the mountains of East Tennessee.

Who exactly are these people we call "spiritual seekers"? Shankara, Augustine, even Jesus himself—each of them, albeit in different ways and for different reasons, suggests that this may not be a question with a definite answer. Or better, to put it in the words of the Priest, "It's not really the right question, is it?"

For "spiritual seekers" is simply *who we are*. We come to our lives with something at stake, with our own questions and confusions, our own hurts and hopes, our own disgust born of desire. No one can determine our most cherished hopes and desires for us, least of all ourselves.

[33] Augustine of Hippo, *On Instructing the Uninstructed,* in Joseph P. Christopher, trans., *St. Augustine: The First Catechetical Instruction,* Ancient Christian Writers 2 (New York and Mahwah: Newman Press, 1946). For a fuller account of these reasons and other elements of this important text, see William Harmless, *Augustine and the Catechumenate* (Collegeville: Liturgical Press, 1995) 107–55, esp. 114–23.

[34] Augustine of Hippo, *On Instructing the Uninstructed* 6.10, in Christopher, 26–27.

[35] Ibid., 8.12, in Christopher, 30–31.

[36] Ibid., 5.9, in Christopher, 24–26.

But Shankara, Augustine and even Jesus himself, again in different ways and for different reasons, seem to hint that, if we are honest and attentive, these very hopes and desires may at some point reach beyond themselves and thereby set us firmly on the path.

For me, in that office in East Tennessee, it was curiosity about this single word "Christ" that brought me to the Priest, along with a healthy dose of anger and indignation at institutional religion. At the time, I might have said that it was my curiosity that brought me to that office in the Catholic student center *despite* the anger and indignation that drove me away. But the Priest pointed out that the curiosity and indignation, like the prospective disciple's disgust and desire, represented flip sides of the same coin. The interesting question wasn't *whether* I was outraged by the persistent scandal and corruption of the institutional Church. Of course, I was! The interesting question was: why? Is it possible that such outrage flowed from an instinct or inchoate desire that I had never really acknowledged? Did I, deep down, suspect that this very institution *might* be, or possibly *should* be, the bearer of a "something more" inseparable from itself?

This is not a question that could be answered in one meeting. I needed another appointment, and then another, and then yet another beyond that, until I had either gained some insight or decided that there was no insight to be found.

In other words, it was time to gather firewood and approach the teacher.

Chapter 2

On Teachers

The Guru

On a late October morning in 1999, almost ten years after my baptism in the Church, I sat dripping in a foldout chair in the foyer of a simple apartment in the district of Abhirampuram in Chennai, India. I had planned badly, in every respect. My poncho *had* kept out some of the rain, but only at the price of retaining heat. How much of the puddle forming beneath my chair was rain and how much was sweat was anybody's guess. I had perhaps one dry notebook in my bag, but I would have to borrow a pen. When I had shown up at the door minutes earlier, the white-clad brahmachari—a lifelong student and devotee of the Guru—had taken one look at me and gestured to the chair, "Just a moment, please; he will be with you soon." He clearly knew who I was: the Guru was expecting me. So much for first impressions.

An elderly woman sat at the other end of the row of chairs, presumably waiting to offer her respects. Her polite smile in my direction was surely well-meant, but in my imagination it spoke volumes: "What a clown!" In India less than a week, I concluded morosely, and I was already making a fool of myself in the home of the very person for whom I had traveled all this way in the first place.

Eventually, the brahmachari gestured to me, and I rose, waterlogged socks squishing a bit beneath me. I was so excruciatingly self-conscious that I remember very little of my first meeting with the Guru. I'm sure that I offered him reverent, if clumsy, salutations. I think he asked me to tell him about my research, and particularly about my interest in Shankara's *A Thousand Teachings,* for which I had requested instruction some months before. I believe a conversation ensued about whether my Sanskrit had progressed as far as I had hoped when I first wrote (it hadn't) and whether I had made time to visit *his* teacher's institute in Pennsylvania (thankfully, I had). I know that my head was swimming with financial concerns: should I offer to pay him? Or should I make a donation later? What is the protocol here?

At some point—and this I remember very well—the Guru just cut my fumbling explanations short. "There is something you need to know," he said, leaning back from his small desk and flashing a wide smile. "I am a Swami, a guru. I don't need anything from you. I have no expectations of you." He paused, and I wondered where he was going with his dramatic pronouncement. He surprised me. "So you should feel completely free in my presence. You should ask of me whatever it is that you wish to know, bring up any topic you wish to discuss. You should be free."

From that point onward we were all business. We read together three or four days every week. We moved slowly, verse by verse. He explained the meaning of each text, and whenever I had questions he answered them without missing a beat, no matter how hard I pushed the issue at hand. When I felt impelled to share my spiritual biography with him about a month into the study, he was very pleased to listen and even responded in kind—but he never indicated that this was at all necessary for our study. When I wanted to discuss how Shankara's teaching intersected with my Christian faith, he engaged in discussion and even asked me to clarify points about Christianity that puzzled him—but he allowed me to initiate the conversation. When, as I began to trust him more, I decided to reveal my confusions about vocation and life in the wake of Egerton's and Jennifer's sudden and pointless deaths, he listened carefully and offered helpful reflections—but his disposition toward me was not significantly altered by the encounter. And we always, always returned to the text. The only interruptions were the occasional devotees who arrived to offer salutations, reverently bowing or even throwing themselves prostrate before the Guru. Often he would, in turn, offer each of them a pinch of holy ash as *prasada,* a gift from the Lord.

It took me some time to realize that these momentary "interruptions," as awkward as they were for me as a product of American culture, aptly symbolized what was happening all of the time in the Guru's presence. It was all *prasada:* the teaching, the discussion, the sensitive reflections. Thoroughly steeped in the Hindu tradition of Advaita Vedanta and having assimilated its teaching on the self, this teacher understood that he had nothing left to achieve, nothing to acquire, nothing to "work out" in his relationships with students. As a result, he could offer his attention and his teaching freely, as the gifts that they were.

Yet I too had been pronounced "free." I had come as a spiritual seeker, as a person with something at stake. To be sure, I was no longer quite the same seeker whom the Priest had met in that small office in East Tennessee. I had received Christ as my light and my hope for one thing, and I had also accumulated five years of graduate theological study. Nevertheless, I continued to be driven by much the same disgust and desire that had brought me to the Church in the first place, and I was occupied by many of the same questions and confusions about religious institutions. It was not an accident that I had come to India asking about the status and authority of the spiritual teacher in Advaita tradition. In the process, I found myself in the presence of just such a spiritual teacher in the flesh.

And, perhaps a bit surprisingly, I slowly discovered that he was also *my* teacher, that he had something to teach me about my Church and the journey I was taking inside and outside its walls. In short, he helped redefine whatever I might mean by "teacher," "authority," or even "institution" in the first place. So, in another of those moments of clarity that have framed my life and journey of faith, I can honestly say that nothing ever will be quite the same.

A First Hurdle

Before going further, we should perhaps state the obvious. For many people—including me, as it happens—the question of "teachers" and especially "teaching authority" in the spiritual journey is a tough one.

Why is this? Why does this issue either fall barren or strike sparks of controversy for so many members of our societies? There are many possible answers to this question, but a number of them seem a little too easy, at least for my sensibility. For example, one of my graduate school professors used to deplore the tendency of "we moderns," accustomed as we are to scientific methods of inquiry, to acknowledge the possibility of certain knowledge beyond the reach of these methods. This assessment has merit, I think, but it is just too easy to represent a final or enduring answer to the question. Some Indians of my acquaintance seem to think that it is primarily a cultural issue: since American structures of family and civil society are ever more rapidly eroding in the face of rampant individualism, it is not surprising that respect for spiritual teachers is also becoming ever more tenuous. As a member of "generation X," I'm somewhat defensive about this suggestion, but I suppose I have to acknowledge that it contains more than a grain of truth. Nevertheless, it also seems too easy, possibly even superficial.

Finally, we might point to the manifold and highly publicized failures of many in authority—religious or otherwise—to honor the trust that others place in them. To cite just one prominent and recent example: when I first moved to New England as a graduate student in the early '90s, the cardinal archbishop of Boston represented as powerful a symbol of teaching authority as could probably be found in the American Catholic Church. Ten short years later, the fallout of yet another sexual abuse crisis squarely at his feet, the same archbishop emerged as a preeminent and widely criticized symbol of broken trust.[1] If these are the spiritual teachers we have trusted in the past, we may perhaps be forgiven for approaching the issue of "teachers" and especially "teaching authority" with tremendous cynicism.

Despite the strength of this last objection, particularly in the cases of those who have been personally injured, it still rings hollow as a refutation of "teachers" in general. Not all teachers break the trust we place in them—even in the Church!—and not all authority is misused. The truth, as one might expect, is just not that simple.

So where can we look for a better answer? With each passing year, I become more convinced that we should look to the nature of the spiritual quest itself. For the teacher's place and function within this quest is fraught with paradox. This emerges most clearly, perhaps, with reference to Shankara's prospective disciple, from the previous chapter. If

---

[1] For a deeper exploration of this and other cases of broken trust in the Catholic Church, see especially Donald Cozzens, *Sacred Silence: Denial and the Crisis in the Church* (Collegeville: Liturgical Press, 2002).

this seeker conceives a sense of disgust for "the worlds as built by rites," which Shankara interprets as the universe envisioned by the Vedic scriptures, why on earth would such a person immediately seek out a teacher well versed in these same Vedas? Or, to generalize and extrapolate a bit, if our deepest hopes and desires press us beyond what the objects and conventions of ordinary life can reach, if we find ourselves seeking a "something more," a divine reality that is more permanent and fulfilling than anything this world can provide, why look for it in another human being? Isn't that just substituting one limited object in the world for another one? If so, then even legitimate attachment to a teacher or appropriate submission to teaching authority might deepen the problem, rather than offering a solution. We still find ourselves seeking for what is ultimate and enduring in the realm of those things that are neither ultimate nor enduring in and of themselves.

It's a tough question all right.

Our Christian bishop seemed to think so. Indeed, the paradoxical status and function of the teacher and teaching authority was an issue that occupied a great deal of Augustine's attention, particularly in the period immediately after his baptism. At one extreme, in a work simply entitled *The Teacher,* he argues that there is only one authentic teacher, divine Wisdom herself, intimately present to the heart and mind of each and every human person.[2] Spirituality consists, above all, in redirecting our attention and "tuning in" to what this interior and innate Wisdom has to tell us.

At the other extreme, in such works as *On the Usefulness of Belief,* Augustine readily commends submission to a very external authority he accepted on his own spiritual journey:

> If, therefore, your experience has been [like mine], and you have been similarly anxious about your soul, if now at last you see you have been sufficiently tossed about and wish to bring your toils to an end, follow the way of the Catholic discipline which has been derived from Christ himself and has come down to us through the apostles, and by us will be passed on to posterity.[3]

Ultimately, for Augustine, these opposite extremes are held together in the person of Jesus of Nazareth, divine Wisdom in the flesh, who

---

[2] Augustine of Hippo, *The Teacher,* esp. 11.38–14.46, in Burleigh, 95–101.
[3] Augustine of Hippo, *On the Usefulness of Belief* 8.20, in Burleigh, 307.

culminates and encapsulates a sacred strand of human history stretching into the remote past and reaching forward into present and future.[4] The extraordinary narrative recorded above all in the Christian Scriptures—Wisdom embodied and communicated to the world—acts like a kind of mirror, revealing through its vast array of very human characters and events our own shattered expectations and unquenchable desires . . . along with the true God, who transforms these expectations and meets us in these desires. The narrative reflects us back to ourselves, not only as the spiritual seekers we are, but as seekers already in the intimate and loving presence of the One in whom all our desiring might finally come to rest. This intimate and loving presence is what we have been seeking outside of ourselves all this time, when in truth it has never been away from us.

Augustine's vision of the spiritual journey, in which seekers return to themselves precisely in and through their contact with the great canvas of God's work across history, is both brilliant and profound. It is also a bit circular, and, as Augustine would be the first to admit, it rests upon a host of presuppositions. How do we encounter sacred history and its Wisdom in the first place? How do we know that what it reflects back to us is true? How and where, in other words, do we enter this circle of personal and scriptural revelation? Augustine's reply to such questions is deceptively simple.

We start with belief.

The answer is deceptive only because it appears to introduce belief as something new or different from what we might expect. If one were to conclude that such a call for belief *is* something entirely new, however, Augustine might wave his finger in our direction with an *"au contraire,"* or better, *"sed contra."* Belief, as such, is already and always a persistent feature of our daily lives. Indeed, many of the things we profess to know we have actually only received in a mediated way, through common knowledge, a textbook, or some other reliable witness.[5]

---

[4] E.g. Augustine of Hippo, *On the Usefulness of Belief* 14.30–18.36, in Burleigh, 316–23. Cf. Augustine of Hippo, *On True Religion* 1.1–23.44, in Burleigh, 225–47. Also see R. A. Markus, *Saeculum: History and Society in the Theology of St. Augustine,* rev. ed. (Cambridge: Cambridge University Press, 1988).

[5] Although I have supplied my own examples, the following discussion is largely dependent upon the treatment of belief in Eugene TeSelle, *Augustine the Theologian* (New York: Herder and Herder, 1970), esp. 127–29. See also Augustine of Hippo, *Eighty-Three Different Questions* 48, in David L. Mosher, trans., *Saint Augustine: Eighty-Three Different Questions,* Fathers of the Church 70 (Washington, D.C.: The Catholic University of America Press,

Take history for example. When I first moved to Athens as an adolescent, I was immediately enrolled in a required eighth-grade course in Georgia history, easily one of my favorite classes of all time. Although I have by now forgotten much of what I learned, at the time it would never have occurred to me to question whether I was acquiring real facts about a state and region I was even then beginning to love. But was what I learned actually "knowledge" in the strictest sense of that term? Not without a good measure of belief, that's for sure. Given time, equipment, and a crack team of geographers, I suppose I could ascertain for myself that Georgia is the largest U.S. state east of the Mississippi. What about the 1733 arrival at Savannah of a group of English settlers under the leadership of James Edward Oglethorpe? Well, if I distrusted the textbook we used, I might unearth a variety of primary sources: journals, ship inventories, legal documents related to land claims, and the like. At some point, however, I would have to judge whether the statements in *these documents* could be considered reliable. Since I was not personally waiting on the Georgia coast in 1733 to witness these events, my only access to them is through belief in the testimony of others.

We seem to be on firmer ground with the natural sciences. There, at least in the abstract, most of what we receive on the testimony of others might eventually be directly verified. If I read about reflection and refraction of light in a physics textbook, for example, I can immediately pull out a magnifying glass or prism to test some of the things I have read. But then there is something like Einstein's famous formula, $E = mc^2$. On a really good day, I might be able to define all of the terms in this equation and speak in vague detail about how they relate to the Special and General Theories of Relativity. I used to study and then to teach mathematics, yet I have never retraced for myself the proofs and derivations by which Einstein produced this important equation. If I'm honest with myself, I have to admit that it's unlikely I ever will, occupied as I now am teaching religion and writing about spirituality. Finally, despite attentive visits to several Museums of Science and Technology, I persist in my ignorance about how Einstein's theories have been supported by observation and empirical verification. I *believe* that they have been so verified, and so I also accept his equation as a

1982) 83; and Gerald Bonner, *St. Augustine of Hippo: Life and Controversies*, rev. ed. (Norwich: Canterbury Press Norwich, 1986) esp. 224–27.

"fact," a generally reliable and accurate description of the world in which we live.

In our day-to-day life, there is no avoiding belief. The vast majority of what we "know" comes to us, not through our own experience, but through the witness of others whom we consider trustworthy. Imagining our lives any other way leads us to various kinds of absurdity—denying the existence of cholesterol or the moons of Jupiter perhaps, or really, *really* wishing we could have had the foresight to take a quick tissue sample on the way out of the womb so as to later verify our mothers' claims to have given us birth. A life that is not firmly grounded in a good deal of appropriate belief is not the life of a healthy, well-adjusted human being.

For this reason, when Augustine commends belief as an appropriate next step for those who have recognized themselves as seekers, he does not judge that he is demanding anything extraordinary or even all that unusual. Quite the opposite. We are, as we discovered in the previous chapter, spiritual seekers in and through our most cherished hopes and desires, not somehow *outside* or *despite* them. So, for Augustine, it just stands to reason that we should not expect to arrive at the truth to which these cherished hopes and desires ultimately refer in a way that is somehow outside the ordinary ways we learn *anything* of value. In fact, he claims, we will arrive at this truth in *exactly* the same way we arrive at the vast majority of what we generally accept as certain knowledge.

That is, we will start with belief.

Friendship and Fluency

Thus far we have been discussing belief in the abstract, as a characteristic of ordinary life and as an important step in the spiritual journey. Based on our personal experiences, we might anticipate a series of further leaps that specify the type and content of belief in no uncertain terms: "Do you *believe* in Jesus Christ as your personal Lord and Savior?" "Do you *believe* that God will forgive your sins?" "Repent, and *believe!*" If we have never heard clarion calls like these, we simply haven't been spending enough time at outdoor concerts or other crowded public events.

Now, it should hopefully come as no surprise that I am deeply sympathetic with these evangelical charges, even if I often end up either ignoring or arguing with the preachers from whom they issue. Christ as Lord and Savior, forgiveness of sins, the value of repentance—these are truths I affirm and happily share with others.

Despite my sympathy and shared faith, however, I cannot restrain myself from setting such evangelical demands for belief, thrown indiscriminately at strangers in a milling crowd, against the example of a person like the Guru. It's not that the Guru never presumed or encouraged belief, to be sure. On the contrary, he would readily commend faith in the Hindu scriptures, in doctrines like reincarnation, and especially in the Lord. Even the liberating truth of the self, as I understand it, requires initial assent before it can blossom as firm conviction and certain knowledge. What appeared to set the Guru apart from the Christian proselytizer, however, was this: it would be unthinkable for the Guru to *demand* such belief, no matter how essential it might be. Indeed, the Guru's teaching seemed to presume that, in the presence of the right teacher, the beliefs appropriate to spiritual pursuit have a natural, almost spontaneous quality about them. They flow seamlessly from a deep sense of recognition that this teacher, here and now, can offer reliable testimony and guidance on my spiritual path.

The naturalness and spontaneity of belief finds apt expression in two further analogies employed by Augustine to highlight the importance of teachers and teaching tradition. The first is the experience of intimate friendship.[6] Augustine notes that true friendship, like Oglethorpe's arrival on the Georgia coast, is not something that can be directly observed. We can observe *actions* and draw reasonable conclusions from them, to be sure, but the inner dispositions of other persons are not themselves available for inspection. In friendship, we always risk some level of belief and trust in the goodwill of another. Sometimes, it is true, such trust turns out to be misplaced. And inevitably, precisely because we may have been betrayed or hurt in the past, it will be much more difficult for some than for others. Refusal to extend trust at all or in any circumstances, however, almost invariably brings deeper hurt and social isolation.

This leads to Augustine's second analogy, in which a refusal to extend trust is virtually identical to isolation. For there is perhaps no

---

[6] See especially Augustine of Hippo, *On Faith in Things Unseen* 1.2–3.5, in Ludwig Schopp and others, trans., *Writings of Saint Augustine, Vol. 2*, Fathers of the Church 2 (New York: Cima Publishing Co., 1947) 452–56.

greater social force connecting persons to one another than language, and we learn language exclusively through the mediation of others whom we trust.[7] This was dramatically underscored for me during a trip to Tokyo a few years back. Never before or since this trip have I encountered a community of persons more supportive of my fumbling attempts with their native language. From the family I was visiting to the teller at the local bank, nearly everyone I encountered wanted to compliment me on my Japanese and encourage me to improve. Despite my lack of formal training, in two short months my spoken Japanese (pathetic though it nevertheless remained) had easily outstripped my facility with spoken German, which I had studied in college for the better part of three years. The reason for this is well known, I'm sure, to language educators: I was learning Japanese the way I had learned English, by listening, interacting directly with a variety of native speakers, and implicitly, *spontaneously* trusting them not to lead me astray.

It might not be too great a stretch to suggest that, for Augustine in his early years, the spiritual journey can be fruitfully compared to learning a language or cultivating a friendship. It requires at least tentative belief in what we cannot perceive directly and do not yet know for ourselves, and it proceeds by means of our interactions with other people. As we gain in trust and lived experience, we acquire a kind of spiritual vocabulary for ourselves as seekers and also for what we seek. It is not a matter of *demanding* belief, but of inviting it, nurturing it and communicating the authentic life—spiritual friendship or fluency—toward which such belief naturally tends. In the presence of the right teacher, nothing could be more reasonable and appropriate.

Meeting on the Journey

The key term in all of this may be "presence." Trust, belief, the spiritual friendship or fluency that proceeds from belief—these, I have suggested, happen in the *presence* of the right teacher. Generally speaking, we don't make or keep friends in the absence of significant personal contact. Similarly, with rare exceptions, we don't acquire fluency with a

[7] See Saint Augustine of Hippo, *On Christian Doctrine*, Prologue 4–5, in D. W. Robertson Jr., *Saint Augustine: On Christian Doctrine* (Upper Saddle River: Prentice Hall, 1958) 4–5.

language merely by memorizing vocabulary and grammar from a text-book. We learn through sustained practice, ideally in the presence of at least one other person who has progressed further in the language than we have. The trust that grounds friendship or fluency ordinarily requires at least some level of personal presence and attention.

If this holds true in the cases of friendship and fluency, we might venture to guess, how much more should it hold true for the spiritual journey? If we have recognized ourselves as true seekers, full of our own questions and confusions, our own hurts and hopes, our own disgust born of desire, we are not, it seems to me, looking for a set of propositions like "Jesus is Lord and Savior." Propositions there may well be, even propositions that are *true* and *revealing* about the fundamental nature of our search. But such propositions, like the vocabulary and grammar of a language, acquire real significance in yet another "something more" inseparable from themselves: actual communication, fluency, a revolution in how we describe things in the world, a new vision of this world and our place in it. For this, we need someone who can not only transmit the propositions, but also show us the way. And this would seem to require someone who is willing and ready to be *present*, to sit with us for a while on the journey.

As it happens, one of my favorite passages from the Christian Gospels begins with a teacher who quite literally chooses to sit for a while on a journey:

> . . . [Jesus] left Judea and started back to Galilee. But he had to go through Samaria. So he came to a Samaritan city called Sychar, near the plot of ground that Jacob had given to his son Joseph. Jacob's well was there, and Jesus, tired out by his journey, was sitting by the well. It was about noon (John 4:3-6).

Now, we know from our previous glance at the Fourth Gospel in the introduction that the final, exceedingly pedestrian statement in this passage—"It was about noon"—could easily be read as a cue that we are about to witness one of those thoroughly ordinary, yet simultaneously extraordinary and earth-shaking events that define the Gospel as a whole. We are further primed by the fact that Jesus is sitting, not at any old well, but at one named after Jacob, father of the nation and religion that bears another name given to this same Jacob by God the divine Self: "Israel." Something is bound to happen.

We are not left disappointed: "A Samaritan woman came to draw water, and Jesus said to her, 'Give me a drink.' [For] his disciples had gone to the city to buy food" (vv. 7-8). There is nothing very unusual about this request. Jesus is sitting alone and, as we know from the previous passage, it's the middle of what is probably a scorcher of a day. A woman comes along, water jar in hand. If Jesus wants a drink, this is his chance.

On the face of it, then, this situation is thoroughly ordinary. At the same time, it is quite unusual. It represents a breach of decorum for one thing, as implied by the woman's immediate response: "How is it that you, a Jew, ask a drink of me, a woman of Samaria?" (v. 9a). It would be rash, from this isolated statement, to offer sweeping generalizations about first-century Jewish attitudes toward women or Samaritans. Instead, we may simply note that, from this woman's experience and point of view (a view which will later be confirmed in the disciples' own reactions to her in verse 27), Jesus appears to violate convention by speaking to her. He transgresses the boundaries that she would have presumed from him, boundaries that would insulate women from men, Jews from Samaritans. This makes his request somewhat extraordinary.

But not nearly as extraordinary as the lofty spiritual discourses that follow (vv. 10-26). What begins as a request for water opens into an extended discussion of eternal life (v. 14), spiritual worship (vv. 23-24), and the Messiah (v. 25). As a professional theologian, I possess an almost instinctive urge to distill from this discussion a series of claims or propositions about salvation, about worship, and about Jesus himself. As important as such claims might be, however, it is every bit as important to notice how they arise: in and through the ebb and flow of a very personal, even intimate conversation. The Samaritan woman asks why Jesus is willing to request a drink from her, and Jesus reveals that he can give her "living water" (vv. 9-10). Jesus asks after her husband, and her honest reply leads to the revelation that she has had a number of marital, and at least one extramarital, relationships (vv. 16-18). The woman asks about the rival claims of Jerusalem and Mount Gerizim as places of worship, and Jesus commends worship "in spirit and truth" (vv. 20, 24). The woman confesses her expectations for a coming Messiah, and Jesus replies, "I am he," or, more literally, "I AM," a traditional self-designation of God (vv. 25-26). At each step, the Samaritan woman risks a bit more of herself—her history, her questions, her hopes and expectations—and at each step Jesus responds, unfolding not merely a series of propositions about the spiritual life, but also himself as bearer and revelation of the life he describes. He does not just tell her *what* to believe. He reveals in his person the very life nourished by such belief.

This is extraordinary indeed. What I find *most* extraordinary about this passage, however, is the way that the Samaritan woman will later characterize their encounter to the denizens of Sychar: "Come and see a man who has told me everything I have ever done!" (v. 28). This is most curious to me, since in the actual discourses Jesus speaks only briefly about her life and about only one feature of it: her relationships with men (vv. 17-18). This is *everything* she has ever done? Not likely.

Perhaps there is another way to understand the Samaritan woman's statement. What, we can ask, is actually revealed by the fact that she had five previous husbands and is now living with someone who is not her husband (v. 18)? Sexual immorality? Maybe, maybe not. Marriages end in many different ways, including death and abandonment. So, when I read this revelation about the Samaritan woman's life, I am at most half-convinced that her character has been at all impugned. More certain, at least in my mind, is the fact that she has seen more than her share of suffering. She has come to this well, dragging a water jar, filled with her own hurts, her own questions, perhaps also her own dignity and strength as one who has seen the worst the world has to offer and yet emerged intact. She is not one easily taken in by false promises. She has seen *those* before, and aplenty.

And what happens? She meets a teacher who also meets with her, revealing who she is and what she has been seeking all this time: the *culmination* of everything she has ever done, desired, or hoped for. She risks only a bit of herself at a time, which is perfectly natural. He responds in kind, sometimes introducing new truths and other times gently correcting the half-truths that have heretofore defined her life. In doing both, however, he sits for a while and makes himself present to her.

The outcome of this conversation reverberates far beyond Jacob's well:

> Many Samaritans from that city believed in [Jesus] because of the woman's testimony, "He told me everything I have ever done." So when the Samaritans came to him, they asked him to stay with them; and he stayed there two days. And many more believed because of his word. They said to the woman, "It is no

longer because of what you said that we believe, for we have heard for ourselves, and we know that this is truly the Savior of the world" (John 4:39-42).

The Samaritan woman, who compares rather favorably to Peter and the other disciples in this regard, does not miss a beat. She immediately follows her teacher's own example: she points the way, brings these other seekers into Jesus' presence, and thereby opens the door for their initial belief to blossom as intimate knowledge. The divine source and end of spiritual pursuit in the Fourth Gospel—Jesus himself—is now inseparable from the Samaritan woman *herself* as she communicates its message and its new life to others.

An Ideal Teacher?

Reading the story of the Samaritan woman, I always feel a small stab of envy. When the residents of Sychar hear the testimony of this model teacher, who outstrips even the twelve disciles in her ability to assimilate Jesus' teaching and communicate it to others, these seekers are immediately brought into the very tangible presence of Jesus himself. We contemporary seekers are, on the other hand, seemingly forced to rely more heavily on testimony alone. Even Jesus' response to "Doubting Thomas" much later in the Fourth Gospel—"Blessed are those who have not seen and yet have come to believe" (John 20:29)—doesn't resolve the dilemma. In the light of so many conflicting calls for belief from various Christian groups, not to mention a vast array of other religious traditions, spiritual paths, and secular ideologies, whose testimony can we trust? Who are the Samaritan women in our contemporary world, and how do they bring us into the intimate presence of the source and end of our spiritual striving?

We have already begun to answer this question with reference to Jesus and the Samaritan woman themselves. The right teacher will be someone who can meet us and be present to us, wherever we happen to be coming from. This teacher may well request or presume belief and trust on our part, but such belief will not rest content with bare faith claims or propositions. It will look to the person of the teacher herself, not only for her message but also for the ways in which she embodies this message and the life promised by it. In and through our personal contact with such a teacher, we will seek a spiritual grammar and fluency, a new sense of relationship that just might come to redefine our lives and our striving until we strive no more.

This is obviously a tall order. Nevertheless, our Hindu teacher Adi Shankaracharya, no less than our Christian bishop, clearly believed that it does not lie outside the realm of possibility.

In *A Thousand Teachings,* as already noted in the previous chapter, Shankara cites an important passage from the Upanishads to describe the "moment of clarity" that defines the spiritual seeker. This passage is especially significant, however, because it also mentions the two most important qualifications of the ideal teacher. Such a person is both *shrotriya,* "well-versed in the Vedas," and *brahmanishtha,* "focused on *brahman.*"[8] The latter term reappears as a description of the teacher in the second prose chapter of *A Thousand Teachings,* along with two others: *brahmana,* a "Brahmin" or more probably a "knower of *brahman,*" and *sukham asina,* "sitting at ease."[9] Elsewhere in this work Shankara expands considerably on these qualifications:

> The teacher is one who is endowed with the power of furnishing arguments pro and con, of understanding questions and remembering them, who possesses tranquility, self-control, compassion and a desire to help others, who is versed in the scriptures and unattached to enjoyments both seen and unseen, who has renounced the means to all kinds of actions, is a knower of *brahman* and established in *brahman,* is never a transgressor of the rules of conduct, and who is devoid of shortcomings such as ostentation, pride, deceit, cunning, fraud, jealousy, falsehood, egotism and attachment. He has the sole aim of helping others and a desire to impart the knowledge of *brahman* only.[10]

These descriptions, we see, combine formal qualifications, such as a firm grounding in the Vedic scriptures, with desirable personal qualities and virtues, including, above all, compassion.[11] If we recognize someone

---

[8] Mundaka Upanishad 1.2.12, in Olivelle, *Upanisads,* 270. See also William Cenkner, *A Tradition of Teachers: Sankara and the Jagadgurus Today* (Delhi: Motilal Banarsidas Publishers, 1983, 1995) 8–10.

[9] Shankara, *A Thousand Teachings,* Prose Portion 2.45, in Jagadananda, 33–34.

[10] Ibid., Prose Portion 1.6, in Jagadananda, 5 (slightly modified).

[11] See J. G. Suthren Hirst, "The Place of Teaching Techniques in Samkara's Theology," *Journal of Indian Philosophy* 18 (1990) 130–31.

as *our* teacher, Shankara implies, it is because we recognize in her the knowledge, the spiritual maturity, and even the interpretive skills required to disclose what we are seeking and who it is we are seeking to become.

Shankara's vision of the teacher may seem a bit idealized, but that may also be part of his point. His descriptions begin with an assumption that the ideal teacher truly knows *brahman*, the divine Self at the root of all creation, and thus fully embodies the source and end of spiritual life; other characteristics, from facility with scripture to a personal demeanor of comfort and compassion, follow from this interior knowledge itself. However, since seekers, as Shankara himself will readily concede, have no direct access to the teacher's knowledge and innermost disposition,[12] we have to base our initial judgments upon externals. The "idealized teacher" in Shankara's description then serves as a reliable if not infallible guide for finding a teacher who may (or may not) actually *be* ideal. Informed and shaped by such guidelines, we are empowered to make the best judgments we can, given the limitations of our circumstances. Just as with friendship and other relationships, there is a persistent and unavoidable element of risk.

But not blind risk. We may not know, at least not without significant and sustained contact, the interior detachment or personal virtue of any teacher we encounter. We may *never* know for sure whether this teacher has been truly and thoroughly reshaped by that divine reality we have come to seek in and though spiritual instruction. We can, however, look for a person who exhibits external signs of compassion and humility, someone whose teaching is firmly grounded in a well-attested scriptural tradition and directed toward the highest good of others. Finally, Shankara suggests, we can look for someone who generally sits at ease, without evident fear or defensiveness.

This final stipulation may seem superficial, but I believe it is the most critical of all. We can perhaps see its importance with reference to our Christian bishop Augustine's description of someone he considered to be a poor, inadequate teacher:

---

[12] See especially Shankara, Commentary on Bhagavad-Gita 14.22, in A. G. Krishna Warrier, trans., *Srimad Bhagavad Gita Bhasya of Sri Sankaracarya, With Text and English Translation* (Madras: Sri Ramakrishna Math, 1983) 484: "The sage's attitude to these [mental] states is not obvious to the outsider; rather, being evident only to the self, the sage alone may perceive his inner marks. An outsider, of course, cannot discern the inwardly felt aversion and attachment."

> For a long time I had eagerly awaited Faustus. When he came, I was delighted by the force and feeling he brought to his discourse and by the fitting language which flowed with facility to clothe his ideas. . . . But I was disappointed that in the public assembly of his audience I was not allowed to put a question, and to share with him the perplexing questions disturbing me, by informal conference and by the give and take of argument.[13]

Later Augustine would arrange such an informal conference and confirm that no credible responses were forthcoming; he credits Faustus for, at least, being honest about his ignorance and inability to reach beyond the most superficial precepts of his Manichee faith.[14] But Augustine demanded more than this. Never a fan of fruitless controversy, he nevertheless thought that authentic teachers should openly and comfortably entertain questions by the "give and take of argument." *Unquestioning* belief is, for Augustine no less than for Shankara, not conducive to an authentic spiritual life, and those who demand such belief only prove themselves uncomfortable and insecure.

At a minimum, then, I think that the ideal teacher is someone who reveals a high level of comfort with difficult questions. We may not get simple or direct answers from such teachers, to be sure. We may even discover that some of the questions we are asking are the wrong ones. But to assert, as some teachers have done throughout history and continue to do even today, that earnest questioning is incompatible with authentic belief betrays the very nature of spiritual pursuit and, most importantly, of ourselves as seekers. We come with our own questions and confusions, and we need teachers who can be comfortable with them, *even if* simple answers may not be immediately forthcoming.

Indeed simple "answers," as such, may not be forthcoming at all. And perhaps this, too, is part of Shankara's point.

Inessential and Indispensable

Now, finally, we arrive at an important observation that may be a bit of a kicker for some: it seems very likely, at least to me, that our deepest questionings and desires do not lend themselves to simple formulas, to

---

[13] Augustine of Hippo, *Confessions* 5.6.11, in Chadwick, 78.
[14] Ibid., 5.6.11–7.12, in Chadwick, 78–79.

bland assurances, or indeed to *any* solutions we might expect or imagine on our own. Instead, just as in friendship or fluency, our spiritual journey may well yield its fruit only through sustained commitment with one or more teachers who are also committed to us.

This is quite a claim, and I have offered no real argument to support it. Nevertheless, if there is one thing upon which Augustine, Shankara, and the author of the Fourth Gospel would completely agree, it is probably this: without the intervention of a credible teacher or spiritual guide, we live in a state of bondage. Augustine, Shankara, and the author of the Fourth Gospel differ in rather significant ways about the particulars of our situation, to be sure. How and why are we in bondage? What *exactly* is required to set us free? On these points they differ, and their differences are not wisely ignored. Yet all three—along with not a small number of other Hindus and Christians, at the very least—view the disgust and desire of spiritual seekers as our first, inchoate reminders of something we have inexplicably forgotten. The spiritual horizon is much broader and brighter than we could ever have hoped or imagined, and yet we have been well trained to keep our gazes fixed upon the ground. We need help. We need someone to raise our chins, to catch our glances, and to point out the pink tendrils of dawn.

I recently discovered a beautiful image for this plight, especially as envisioned by Shankara, at the Rodin Museum in Philadelphia, Pennsylvania. As I was walking through this impressive collection of bronzes by the French master Auguste Rodin, my gaze came to rest upon a piece from 1903 titled *The Hand of the Devil Holding Woman*.[15] The title is appropriately descriptive: the artist crafted the figure of a woman held lightly but firmly in the fingers of a large hand. At first glance, there is nothing particularly sinister about the work. Except for its size relative to the person it holds, the hand seems perfectly ordinary. The woman too appears ordinary, even comfortable: a slumbering nude in a semifetal position. If there is anything amiss at all, it might be the way that her face is firmly, almost determinedly pressed into her crossed forearms. Prevented from seeing her face, I am left wondering about

---

[15] An illustration and description of the piece is available in John L. Tancock, *The Sculpture of Auguste Rodin: The Collection of the Rodin Museum, Philadelphia* (Philadelphia: Philadelphia Museum of Art, 1976) 626–27. The analysis of the piece in this work suggests that it was intended as a depiction of the "diabolical" quality of women themselves. While I don't challenge that this may well have been the artist's intention, it seems just as appropriate to interpret this woman as a symbol of all humankind.

her dreams and imaginings, about her losses and deepest questions, about those unsettling suspicions—some of which, no doubt, have long gone unacknowledged—that all is not right with her situation. But what can she do, caught here in the fingers of this great hand? No escape presents itself, so she buries her head more deeply in her arms and tries to go back to sleep.

This sculpture, in turn, reminds me of one of the most stunning scenes from the Wachowski brothers' 1999 blockbuster film *The Matrix*.[16] As those who have seen the film will undoubtedly recall, the "Matrix" is a computer-generated world, designed to occupy the minds and senses of human beings while their bodies are used to generate heat and electricity. At a critical juncture about a third of the way into the movie, the main character—named "Neo" or, in the virtual world, "Mr. Anderson"—disconnects from the Matrix for the first time. Before this point, Neo has always experienced himself as a middle-class American software engineer in a late twentieth-century U.S. city. Now, he suddenly finds himself weak and atrophied, suspended in a translucent vat of pink fluid, with a kind of neural cable in the back of his head. He emerges from his own pod to view a vast farm of such pods. In every direction, he sees rows upon rows of them, each containing a human person slumbering away in the virtual world that has been specifically created to keep them entertained, occupied, and in abject bondage.

Despite the dramatic power of this scene, it is important to note that Neo's transformation neither begins nor ends with a single moment of awakening. In the film, it begins with a question he barely admits to himself: "what is the Matrix?" Then there are email messages and phone calls that confirm his questioning and give him hints about that which he seeks. Finally, there is a guide and mentor named Morpheus, who first offers to show Neo the truth and then—after Neo has made his choice, has taken a "magic pill," and has seen the truth for himself in the climactic, mind-shattering scene described above—physically reconstitutes his real body, educates him in this much bigger world to which he has awakened, and shows him the way to live in it.

Rodin's sculpture and the Wachowskis' film did not arise in cultural vacuums, of course, and so they invite all kinds of connections to images

---

[16] Andy Wachowski and Larry Wachowski, *The Matrix*, dir. Andy Wachowski and Larry Wachowski, 136 min., Warner Studios, 1999.

deeply lodged in the Western mind: the biblical portrait of Eve, the philosopher Plato's famous allegory of the cave, even Lewis Carroll's playful fantasy *Alice in Wonderland*. But both also consciously or unconsciously create bridges to certain stands of Hindu and Buddhist thought when they intimate that our bondage can be represented as a situation of deep sleep. And, as I discover almost every morning, waking up from deep sleep is not something that most of us do entirely on our own. It generally requires recognition, persistence, and a sharp, auditory kick from outside.

In Shankara's Advaita tradition, as we might expect, the process of waking up requires a rather specific commitment to the teaching of a spiritual guide. One way that Shankara illustrates such commitment is through reverent salutations to the teaching tradition at the beginnings and endings of many of his commentaries and other works. Consider the following verses from his *A Thousand Teachings:*

> The self is to be known. It is beyond everything knowable as there exists nothing else except it. I bow down to that pure, all-knowing and all-seeing self which is to be known.
>
> I always bow down to those [teachers] who are conversant with words, sentences and means of knowledge and who, like lamps, have shown clearly [to us] *brahman,* the secret of the Vedas.
>
> I bow down to [my] teacher, whose words fell [into my ears] and destroyed ignorance [in me] like the sun's rays falling on darkness and destroying it.[17]

These introductory verses offer, first, a kind of précis of Advaita teaching. If self-knowledge brings final liberation or salvation from an otherwise endless cycle of births, deaths, and suffering, as Shankara contends with great vigor, then it must be the case that the true self of each and every living being is none other than *brahman,* God the divine Self, the sole reality at the base of all worldly appearances. Since this ultimate identity is not evident from "everything knowable" through our senses—which, on the contrary, suggest that we are distinct, autonomous individuals in the midst of a world also different from ourselves—

---

[17] Shankara, *A Thousand Teachings,* Verse Portion 17.1-3a, in Jagadananda, 191–92 (slightly modified).

we need another, independent "means of knowledge" to wake us up. This we find in the Hindu scriptures, whose highest "secret" meaning is none other than the liberating truth of *advaita* or "nondifference" of self and God.[18]

This, in a nutshell, is Shankara's vision of bondage and liberation. Yet attentive readers will have noticed that, at least in my interpretation, one critical piece seems to be missing: the teacher. Indeed, these verses make it clear that the seeker's commitment to the teacher is of a very particular type. For, when Shankara offers salutations to teachers in general and to his own teacher in particular, he highlights the central *role* they play in bestowing instruction. These teachers are those who interpret the words and sentences of the scriptures so that they are truly meaningful to us, who destroy our inherited and habitual ignorance as the sun dispels the darkness, and who thereby become transparent to and revelatory of that truth we have come to seek. They alone reveal the truth, but they are not to be mistaken for truth itself.

It might not be too inaccurate to suggest that, for Shankara, the teacher is simultaneously inessential and indispensable. *Inessential,* insofar as our commitment to the teacher is not for its own sake, but for the sake of liberation, freedom, thorough fluency in the life and language of the scriptures. *Indispensable,* insofar as liberation requires personal mediation, belief, and trust, someone to sit with us and show us the way—all of those elements we have been considering in this chapter. At the end of the day, even the most ideal teacher is yet another piece of beautiful garbage, whose true significance resides in a "something more" inseparable from herself. The critical difference may be this: the best teacher would be the one who explicitly and without hesitation—in her words, in her presence, in her humility and compassion—points within and beyond herself to that true, divine "something more" that is the only worthy source and end of our commitment.

It is this commitment *itself* that will ground the authority we eventually invest in our teachers' words.

<hr />

[18] See Francis X. Clooney, *Theology after Vedanta: An Experiment in Comparative Theology* (Albany: State University of New York Press, 1993) 92–99; Anantanand Rambachan, *Accomplishing the Accomplished: The Vedas as a Source of Valid Knowledge in Sankara,* Society for Asian and Comparative Philosophy 10 (Honolulu: University of Hawaii Press, 1991) 31–54; and especially Anantanand Rambachan, "Where Words Can Set Free: The Liberating Potency of Vedic Words in the Hermeneutics of Sankara," in *Texts in Context: Traditional Hermeneutics in South Asia,* ed. Jeffrey R. Timm (Albany: State University of New York Press, 1992) 35–42.

Risking Recognition

At this point, we may have completed something like a full circle. Early in this chapter, we noted that the issue of "teachers" and "teaching authority" is a tough one for many members of our societies. Now we have encountered that troubling word "authority" again, as fruit of the commitment that joins seeker to teacher on the spiritual journey. In this context, it is authority that flows from commitment, rather than the other way around. Simultaneously inessential and indispensable in the seeker's spiritual pursuit, even the most exalted teacher speaks a word whose authoritativeness remains firmly rooted in the soil of belief and trust, a field bounded by spiritual pursuit itself. It is only when we come to recognize a teacher as *our* teacher, as a reliable witness to that divine reality we have come through our own hopes and desires to seek, that it becomes possible to speak of this teacher's authority as a necessary feature of our journey.

But this may not be the way we are used to hearing people talk about authority, particularly in religion. Augustine, for example, readily appeals to the more "objective" and institutional authority of the Catholic bishops as successors to the apostles in order to refute opponents,[19] and Shankara for his own part does not hesitate to restrict the authentic Advaita tradition to specific teaching lineages and a particular monastic order.[20] *These* may be the kinds of claims we associate more

---

[19] See, e.g., Augustine of Hippo, *On the Usefulness of Belief* 8.20 and 17.35, in Burleigh, 306–7, 321–22, and Augustine of Hippo, *Against the Epistle of Manicaeus Called Fundamental* 4.5, in Richard Stothert, trans., "St. Augustin: Against the Epistle of Manichaeus Called Fundamental," in *A Select Library of Nicene and Post-Nicene Fathers of the Christian Church, Vol. IV, St. Augustin: The Writings Against the Manichaeans and Against the Donatists*, ed. Philip Schaff, First Series (Buffalo, N.Y.: The Christian Literature Company, 1887) 130–31. Cf. Robert B. Eno, "Doctrinal Authority in Saint Augustine," *Augustinian Studies* 12 (1981) 133–72.

[20] See, e.g., Shankara, Commentary on Chandogya Upanishad 3.23.1 and 8.12.1, in Panoli, vol. 3, 206–7, 899–900; Shankara, Commentary on Brhadaranyaka 3.5.1, in V. Panoli, trans., *Upanishads in Sankara's Own Words*, vol. 4 (Calicut: Mathrubhumi Printing and Publishing Co. Ltd., 1994) 694–95. Cf. Wade H. Dazey, "Tradition and Modernization in the Organization of the Dasanami Samnyasins," in *Monastic Life in the Christian and Hindu Traditions: A Comparative Study*, ed. Austin B. Creel and Vasudha Narayanan (Lewiston/Queenston/Lampeter: Edwin Mellen Press, 1990) 281–321; N. Subrahmanian, "Sankara and the Vedantist Movement," in *Social Contents of Indian Religious Reform Movements*, ed. S. P. Sen (Calcutta: Institute of Historical Studies, 1978) 30–41; Yoshitsugu Sawai, *The Faith of Ascetics and Lay Smartas: A Study of the Sankaran Tradition of Srngeri*, Publications of the

closely with institutional religion, and they may also represent exactly the kind of thinking that creates difficulty for many of us. Such claims may indeed even conjure images of power plays, systemic corruption, or social exclusion . . . and it can hardly be doubted that religious authority has not infrequently been used in precisely these ways.

Still, my own personal difficulty with appeals to apostolic succession or teaching lineage does not lie with the claims themselves, which I judge to be both appropriate and legitimate in their respective contexts. My difficulty is, rather, that such institutional claims seem unlikely to win acceptance without a substantial level of belief, trust, and commitment already in place. In the absence of at least some measure of shared personal commitment and recognition, even the most strenuous assertion of religious authority can expect a rather cold reception.

And rightly so. For, if we come to the spiritual journey with something at stake, it should be very clear by this point that the stakes are raised when we choose to place belief and trust in another person. Some of us may offer such trust easily and without reservation; others may move in short, cautious steps. Either way, it seems to me, there is a substantial and unavoidable element of risk.

Enter a teacher like the Guru, whose personal authority is matched only by the grace and candor with which he exercises such authority. Indeed, at several points in his public lectures the Guru would underscore the need for a teacher in spiritual pursuit through a handy thumbnail formula for such pursuit itself: "systematic and consistent study of the scriptures for a length of time under the guidance of a competent teacher." After repeating the formula a time or two, he would go on to dwell on each individual point. Which scriptures? What counts as "systematic and consistent study"? How long a "length of time"? When he would arrive at the last, absolutely critical feature of the definition— the teacher—the Guru would pause for a moment and offer yet another of his wide, generous smiles: "I *hope* you have found a competent teacher." Laughter would invariably ensue.

Although I have no doubt that the Guru would identify himself as fairly traditional with regard to teachers and teaching lineage, he felt no need to rehearse his qualifications or defend the authority of his words. We students had, perhaps, arrived from many different places and

De Nobili Research Library 19, ed. Gerhard Oberhammer (Vienna: Institut für Indologie der Universität Wien, 1992).

backgrounds, with different questions at the fronts of our minds. Our collective decision to stay and listen, however, demonstrated at least tentative commitment to the value of his teaching. We had already, at some level, recognized him as a competent spiritual teacher. At the same time, even after months or years of study, such recognition would include some measure of hope and uncertainty. So the Guru smiled, looked out into the crowd, and gave honest expression to that same hope and uncertainty.

In my personal judgment, then, strengthened by the example of the Guru, it seems unwise and potentially dishonest to divest the recognition and commitment that joins seeker to teacher entirely of its distinctive combination of belief and trust, hope and profound risk. As seekers, we may recognize our need for a teacher and remain attentive and vigilant to find one. We can fairly easily avoid the extremes: either a kind of spiritual hypochondria that looks for the slightest flaw as a pretext to withhold trust, or a naive credulity that seeks out a teacher on the basis of sheer volume of words or apparent certainty of demeanor. We may find ourselves searching inside a tradition in which we were raised, or we may for some reason be looking elsewhere. But, whatever the complexion of our search, the intricate tapestry of our personal histories, driving concerns and coincidence will always shroud the process with at least a little mystery. I might ask myself *why exactly* it was that I met the Priest before I met the Guru. No answer more compelling than the cultural context of the United States or blind chance comes to mind—in our era of globalization, it obviously could have gone a different way—and yet the consequences in terms of my Christian faith and the journey that flows from it are virtually incalculable. The whole issue is, at the least, puzzling and mysterious.

Nevertheless, as I change into bedclothes and drift off at the end of each day, I have no real doubt that things worked out precisely as they should have. Perhaps this is naïve, and not everyone would or could share my certainty and trust in the vagaries of circumstance that guided each step in my journey. But my certainty remains. Recognition and belief, once offered with a kind of singleness of heart and mind, make their own distinctive claim. They bring us not only to the feet of our spiritual teachers, but also, through those same teachers, to a firmer and clearer perception of ourselves as seekers and also of the fittingness of the very journey we have undertaken. Belief blossoms as conviction, conviction becomes our center of gravity—a knowledge closer and deeper than our own bones and breath. At some point, there is no going back.

Then suddenly or gradually we may discover that we are not now, nor have ever really been, completely alone on the journey. This is when we discover, in and out of our spiritual pursuit, that we are participants in a shared communion.

Chapter 3

On a Shared Communion

Guru, Gurus, and the Bala Vidya Mandir

One thing I will always remember about the Bala Vidya Mandir school in the Adyar district of Chennai, where the Guru offered public classes on the Upanishads and Bhagavad Gita, is the chanting.

> *srutismrtipurananamalayam karunalayam*
> *namami bhagavatpadasankaram lokasankaram*
>
> I salute Shankarabhagavatpada, the abode of the Vedas, other scriptures and epics, the repository of compassion, the one who bestows happiness on the world.[1]

When I set out for class on my stripped-down bicycle every Saturday and Sunday evening, the shadows of trees, of small private residences, and of the huge Ayyappan Temple along San Thome High Road were already growing quite long. Competing with lorries and the ubiquitous auto-rikshaws for a piece of roadway, I would glide across

---

[1] For this and the following verses, I have used the Sanskrit text and, with slight modifications, the English translation of Swami Vagisananda, *Vedic Chanting: Self-Study* (Saylorsburg: Arsha Vidya Gurukulam, n.d.) 2–3. The translations are not strictly literal, but reflect the understanding of the verses in the context of the Arsha Vidya lineage.

the Adyar River Bridge and into the quiet neighborhood of Gandhi Nagar.

By the time I arrived, darkness was thickening around Bala Vidya Mandir. The lecture hall almost exactly resembled my old elementary school gymnasium: a long, bare hall with a small stage at the far end and a few ceiling fans turning lazily well above our heads. If I was early, I could watch the first few devotees arrange the space, rolling grass mats out onto the concrete floor, situating a few rows of folding chairs along the sides, setting up an unobtrusive station with tape recordings of some of the Guru's teachings for sale, along with a small donation jar. Usually, however, by the time I made it to the school grounds all of this was already in place and the hall nearly bursting with women and men from the surrounding community. I would remove my shoes, find a space on the mat, and wait.

At some point, often without any signal I could discern, the chanting would begin. I seldom knew, especially toward the beginning of my stay, which verses were being intoned. Salutations to the guru or to Dakshinamurti (God in the form of the first teacher), prayers for successful study, or simply verses from the chapter we were currently studying—all of these were possible, depending upon the situation. I recently ran across a booklet of prayers with a marked page, so I assume that we sometimes chanted the *Gita-Dhyana-Shloka* before our Gita class. In a sense it didn't matter, at least not to me. Listening to the rise and fall of the Sanskrit syllables, letting go of the traffic and bustle not far outside the door and setting aside other cares, we attempted to ready ourselves, to free our hearts and minds to hear the teaching of freedom.

> *sadasivasamarambham sankaracaryamadhyamam*
> *asmadacaryaparyantam vande guruparamparam*

> I salute the lineage of teachers, beginning with Shiva, the Lord,
> [linked by] Shankaracharya in the middle, and extending down
> to my own teacher.

I don't remember much chanting from my brief stay in the small but significant mountain village of Shringeri, although I'm sure that I must at least have heard chanted hymnodies at the Temple of Shri Sharada Devi—herself an incarnation of the Hindu goddess of wisdom and patroness of Shringeri's authoritative seat of learning, or *matha*. I do remember the amazing train journey from Chennai, across the state of

Tamil Nadu, up the Malabar Coast, and into Karnataka and the city of Mangalore. I *definitely* remember the harrowing bus journey to the rural village, careening around corners on a one-lane road in the mountains of the Western Ghats, horn blasting at full volume to alert anyone who might be coming the other way. And I remember other things, too: the impressive stone Vidyashankar Temple, constructed by the great teacher and administrator Vidyaranya in the fourteenth century; devotees feeding sacred fish on the banks of the Tunga River; a couple of generous families who became my hosts during the visit; a sign on the way into town offering an official welcome on behalf of the Shringeri Lion's Club. But mainly I remember waiting for an audience with His Holiness Jagadguru Sri Bharathi Theertha Mahaswamigal, "Shankaracharya" of the Shringeri *matha* and holy pontiff of the Advaita tradition in south India.[2]

As I recall the event, our group gathered in front of the Shri Sharada Devi Temple, where we were met by a delegate and led across a bridge to a garden outside the official residence. We waited in the shadow of monuments to three of the previous holders of the Shankaracharya office. A few of us spoke quietly about our journeys to this place and our connections to the teaching tradition. There were several lifelong students, a number of religious pilgrims, and even one man who had brought his whole family to seek blessings for the upcoming wedding of his son. All of them endeavored to impress upon me, the obvious outsider, how vital a role the Shankaracharya of Shringeri played in the maintenance of Indian religious and social life.

Then, suddenly, there he was in our midst. In my memory he emerges as a largish man, clothed in a simple ochre robe and wearing the distinctive mark of *smarta* orthodoxy: three lines of ash across his forehead. Other than the small cadre of officials who surrounded him, he could have been any monk in the tradition. He took his place on a small throne, all of us men removed our shirts, and everyone formed a sloppy line to approach, pay our respects, and solicit blessings.

I had carefully prepared for this event and had even figured out how to offer my own greetings and those of the Guru to the Shankaracharya

---

[2] This is actually a somewhat controversial assertion, for the Shankaracharya of Kanchi makes a rival claim to preside over the tradition in south India. See William Cenkner, *A Tradition of Teachers: Sankara and the Jagadgurus Today* (Delhi: Motilal Banarsidas Publishers, 1983, 1995) 114–15, and especially Jonathan Bader, *Conquest of the Four Quarters: Traditional Accounts of the Life of Sankara* (New Delhi: Aditya Prakashan, 2000) 288–303.

in Sanskrit. But when the moment came, I discovered I had nothing to say. I offered the most reverential salutation I could manage, turned and walked back across the river, silently rehearsing the mantras I always recited before study. Somehow, that seemed like enough.

> *isvaro gururatmeti murtibhedavibhagine*
> *vyomavadvyaptadehaya daksinamurtaye namah*

> Salutations to Lord Dakshinamurti, who is all-pervasive like space, but who appears divided as Lord, teacher and self.

Swami Tyagananda made his first impression on me during the opening festivities of the Universal Temple of Shri Ramakrishna in the Mylapore district of Chennai. This event brought out monks in the hundreds, a veritable sea of orange robes in all directions. The crowds were a bit overwhelming, but I gathered my courage and ventured onto the temple grounds with one of my Jesuit hosts to hear a panel on the great nineteenth-century Hindu mystic and saint Ramakrishna's contribution to interreligious dialogue. The day was hot and the sound system too loud, so I found myself drifting a bit.

I quickly became alert when Swami Tyagananda began his part of the program. For he offered a very clear exposition of an Advaita perspective on religious diversity in sympathetic, yet highly critical dialogue with Christian traditions of exclusivism, inclusivism, and pluralism.[3] I was even more pleased when I discovered that this monk had been appointed to serve the Ramakrishna Vedanta Society back in Boston. So I have had opportunities to meet him in person a number of times after that event in Chennai—at the Society, on the Boston College campus, and even at academic conferences in Nashville and Denver. When I wrote to the Guru about this association, tentative as it was, he offered a simple reply: "I am happy to know that you are in touch with the Advaita-*sampradaya*."

Now, the Vedanta Society facility, ensconced in an exclusive Back Bay neighborhood adjacent to Boston University, probably could not differ more from the Shri Sharada Devi Temple in Shringeri. With the exception of some of the religious symbols on the walls and a modest shrine to Shri Ramakrishna himself, it could be any small New England church. Congregants file into rows of creaking wooden chairs, fish

---

[3] We will touch upon these interpretative traditions in the following chapter.

hymnals from beneath the chairs, and, when the organ wheezes to life, croak out a hymn that might itself be a bit on the wooden side. Swami Tyagananda processes into the chapel and takes his seat beside the Ramakrishna shrine. At the conclusion of the introit, however, he doesn't launch right into his sermon. First we chant from a small card distributed at the entrance, a brief salutation to the Lord as pure existence, consciousness and bliss, the origin and goal of all creation. Then, with all of our minds somewhat stilled, the Swami bestows the teaching.

> *gukarastvandhakarasca rukarastannivartakah*
> *andhakaranirodhitvad gururityabhidiyate*

> The letter "gu" stands for darkness and "ru" represents its destruction. A guru is so called because he destroys the darkness.

Back in Chennai, one of the Guru's disciples generally arranged to have him ferried to and from his classes in a massive, clunky Tata Sumo SUV. At some point close to the beginning of our class at Bala Vidya Mandir, students would hear its engine in the lot just outside the hall. A few moments after that telltale roar, the Guru would hurry toward the stage: bare feet, orange robe, a few volumes under his arm. Usually we would all stand. If he was a little late, or if for any other reason we were in the middle of a stanza, however, it was not at all unusual for him to beckon us to remain seated. He would then take his place, adjust the microphone and simply join us in our chanting.

He was the Guru, to be sure, but everyone recognized that there was something greater than an individual guru at work in that room. So we sat together, chanted together, and called to mind that which was drawing us together in the first place.

Together in God's Hand

About five years before he cast the sculpture entitled *The Hand of the Devil Holding Woman,* which we discussed briefly in the previous chapter, Auguste Rodin created a very similar work with a simpler title: *The Hand of God.*[4] Both pieces feature large hands, thoroughly ordinary

---

[4] See John L. Tancock, *The Sculpture of Auguste Rodin: The Collection of the Rodin Museum, Philadelphia* (Philadelphia: Philadelphia Museum of Art, 1976) 622–25.

except for their size, holding human figures. So how do we know that one is the hand of the devil and the other is the hand of God? There is a difference in posture for one thing: whereas the hand of God looks relaxed, with all fingers splayed in support, the devil's hand engages only two fingers and a thumb, clutching its victim in a kind of pinching, talon-like grip. Even more noticeably, the figure held by the devil is completely alone and withdrawn, her face buried in her own forearms. God, on the other hand, holds not one but two individuals, female and male, intertwined and cradling each other's heads, and they are embedded together in what looks like a large clod of dirt, or possibly even modeling clay.

Female, male, and a lump of clay. To rest in the hand of God, the sculpture suggests, is to be firmly rooted in the earth and in the intimate company of others.

Of course, it can hardly be doubted that Rodin crafted this image with the first Genesis creation account in mind, wherein male and female are brought forth together from the emergent world (Gen 1:26-27). But when I see this sculpture, I also think of the Guru's lecture hall, such as it was, at the Bala Vidya Mandir. There we were, legs crossed, rear ends planted firmly on the ground, separated from concrete by only thin mats. In general, women sat on the left and men on the right, but enough couples would sit together on one or the other side that the two groups intermingled without losing their distinctive identities. Female and male, intertwined and planted on the earth, united to one another by the very teaching we had come to hear. Rodin's sculpture becomes, at least in my mind, an apt symbol for the Advaita *sampradaya* or teaching tradition, both as it was embodied at the Bala Vidya Mandir during my brief stay in Chennai and as it reaches to distant places such as the great *matha* at Shringeri or the Ramakrishna Vedanta Society in Boston's Back Bay. In and through this tradition, generation after generation of disciples plant themselves, chant and hear the words of their spiritual teachers, all of them together held firmly in the hand of God.

One of our Hindu teacher's most interesting ways of describing this bond, this loose but supportive hand of God that joins disciples and teachers into a larger whole, is by means of the Sanskrit term *vidya-santati*, perhaps least inaccurately translated as "continuity of knowledge." Shankara writes: "when knowledge is firmly grasped, it conduces to one's own good and to continuity. This continuity of knowledge [*vidya-santati*] is helpful to people, like a boat for one who wants to cross a river."[5] The base noun *santati,* so central to this passage, is derived from the verb *santan* and refers to spreading out, stretching or covering something over, making a connection, or simply having an effect. In its extended usage, it can indicate sustained practice, linear succession, or even family relations.[6] When Shankara uses *vidya-santati* in this short passage, he appears to view it both as a product of knowledge, once it is firmly grasped, and as itself an instrument of good in the world, "like a boat to cross a river." The consequences of spiritual pursuit, it seems, spill out beyond the single moment of recognition, belief and trust that joins seeker to teacher on the spiritual journey. The bond they share, the *santati,* continuity or spreading out of liberating truth, can also be viewed as a reality with its own distinctive character and integrity. *Santati,* as such, is not reducible either to the teacher by herself or to the seekers by themselves, but comprehends both together even as it reaches beyond them to touch other teachers, other seekers, other places and times. This basic idea of *santati*—continuity or spreading out of spiritual pursuit from one place to another, one generation to another—provides, in my judgment, a good point of entry for looking at a religious institution like the Church. Logically speaking, before the Church is a full-blown social institution with laws, regulations, and a formal hierarchy, it is an "institution" in a much more modest, but also more living and profound sense. It is a ripple in the waters of the world, a continuity or spreading out of teachers and seekers who follow in the wake of Jesus the Christ, seekers and teachers who are now intertwined together and planted firmly in the unshaped clay of human life and history. "For where two or three are gathered in my name," Jesus is reported to have said, "I am there among them" (Matt 18:20).

We might, however, push a bit further to ask: gathered together doing what? Praying, meditating, playing board games? Well, based on our two previous chapters, at least one thing these two or three will be doing is teaching and learning, engaging together in a shared effort of spiritual pursuit. And the bond that joins teachers and seekers together this way will undoubtedly reveal something about the broader social body, the *santati* or continuity that is the religious institution.

---

[5] Shankara, *A Thousand Teachings,* Prose Portion 1.3, in Jagadananda, 2–3 (modified). In modifying Jagadananda's translation of *vidya-santati* to read "continuity of knowledge," I am following Mayeda's rendering in *A Thousand Teachings,* 211.

[6] Vaman Shivaram Apte, *The Practical Sanskrit-English Dictionary,* rev. ed. (Delhi: Motilal Banarsidas, 1998) 1617–18.

To see this more clearly, we can return to our Christian bishop's treatise entitled *On Instructing the Uninstructed*, a work which presents, in the words of one notable Augustine scholar, "the Christian message in a nutshell."[7] At its most basic, this message consists of love: God's gift of love in Christ and the twofold human response, a reciprocal love directed toward God the divine Self and a grateful, imitating love directed toward other human beings.[8] For Augustine, such love comprehends and includes ordinary affections, loyalty, possibly even romance, but it also pulls us beyond these more familiar attachments. We love one another precisely because we come to see one another in the context of God's love for all creation, a love bestowed and exemplified in the life, death, and resurrection of Jesus the Christ. It is a *spiritual* love, not in the sense that it eclipses those more immediate, conventional relationships that define so much of our everyday lives, but in the deeper sense that it enlists and refines such loves in light of the source and end of our spiritual pursuit.

Given this message, it should come as no surprise that Augustine encourages Christian teachers to keep love ever before them as they unfold the scriptural narrative. Such love is evident first in the images Augustine uses to describe and encourage such teachers in their work: the hen caring for her brood, a mother chewing food for an infant, a doctor dispensing medicine to a patient, even Christ himself, becoming flesh for our salvation.[9] Augustine also makes a series of practical suggestions to embody this love concretely: adapting the discourse to the particular composition and needs of the audience, pulling some of the more educated hearers aside for a private conference, providing chairs for those who are too exhausted to remain standing—a somewhat unconventional gesture at the time.[10] At each and every step, the teacher's work is saturated by the very love about which she purports to teach.

For Augustine, however, love does not stop there. If love truly motivates the teacher and thoroughly permeates her relationship to the seeker, then it also brings to the surface a deep bond that joins each intimately to the other:

---

[7] William Harmless, *Augustine and the Catechumenate* (Collegeville: Liturgical Press, 1995) 129.

[8] Augustine of Hippo, *On Instructing the Uninstructed* 4.7-8, in Christopher, 21–24.

[9] Ibid., 10.15, 14.21, 15.23, in Christopher, 37–38, 47–48, and 49–51.

[10] Ibid., 8.12, 13.19, 15.23, in Christopher, 30–32, 43–45, and 49–51.

. . . if it be distasteful to us to be repeating over and over things that are familiar and suitable for little children, let us suit ourselves to them with a brother's, a father's, and a mother's love, and when once we are linked to them thus in heart these things will seem new even to us. For so great is the power of sympathy, that when people are affected by us as we speak and we by them as they learn, we dwell each in the other and thus both they, as it were, speak in us what they hear, while we, after a fashion, learn in them what we teach . . . for in proportion as we dwell in them through the bond of love, so do things which were old become new to us also.[11]

This is sound pedagogy, to be sure, an ancient endorsement for what modern educators might call "active learning methods."[12] But it is also more than this. It is nothing less, in fact, than that divine fulfillment we have been seeking: Love Herself, revealed and given shape in Jesus the Christ. This ultimate and transcendent Love does not end with Christ's death and resurrection, but goes on to animate the mutually indwelling sympathy and care that defines Christian instruction and that also, we might guess, defines the broader institution that overflows and spreads out from such instruction. It is, in its own way, a microcosm or miniature image of the Church.

The Ultimate *Team Sport*

When I search my own experience for examples of what the Hindu Shankara might mean by *santati* or the Christian Augustine might mean by a bond of love so deep that teachers learn their own lessons in and through the very seekers who hear them, I invariably think back to my short tenure as a competitive rower.

In the top shelf of a small bedroom closet in my mother's Georgia home there sits an old, haggard shoebox. Inside, nestled among Scouting badges, a plastic bear-claw necklace and even the baptismal candle that commemorates my reception into the Church, there is a first place medal for the Men's Lightweight Four Division of the 1989 Atlanta Rowing Festival. It's one of the few items in that shoebox that I could

[11] Ibid., 12.17, in Christopher, 41.
[12] See Harmless, 135–36; and Walter J. Burghardt, "Catechetics in the Early Church: Program and Psychology," *The Living Light* 1/3 (fall 1964) esp. 110–14.

never credibly claim as *mine*. For, in "sweep" or "crew," as distinct from a more recognizable type of rowing that is sometimes called "sculling," each rower sits atop a narrow shell holding a single long oar with both hands. Bereft of at least one other crew member and the support of *her* oar, a lone rower is doing well if she can simply keep the shell from rolling over. Alone, progress is literally impossible. For this and other reasons, rowers not infrequently refer to crew as "the ultimate team sport."

This is a fine slogan, but it is also an extraordinary and inspiring life experience: moving up and down the slide, feathering the oar as you draw it out of the water, hearing a gentle "plop," and feeling a gentler spray as you reconnect and *pull*. If all four oars do not connect at exactly the same time, you *feel* it. If all four seats don't move up the slide at exactly the same speed, you *feel* it. If someone fails to feather properly, or the boat tips to plunge someone's oar suddenly into the current, you *definitely* feel it. Such "crabs" can bruise limbs, stop the team in its tracks, or even capsize the boat. Most importantly, after months of practice under the guidance of the right coach and coxswain, team members begin to sense one another's every move. And then, if everyone is paying careful attention and the conditions are just right, you no longer feel other team members as different from yourself. The team moves as one living body, sliding, feathering, dropping all four oars into the water with one gentle "plop."

When these moments crystallize, rowing is effortless. The shell feels almost stationary and strangely still as the riverbank and competitors slip away on either side. The crew becomes a perfect harmony of mind and muscle, lungs and limbs.

Such moments of perfect clarity and seamless cooperation were truly sublime. They were also, at least in my experience, fairly rare. They were built upon consistent effort and dedication: dragging ourselves out of bed, pulling on clothes that were never quite warm enough, and trudging down to the banks of the Tennessee River no later than 6:00 a.m. at least five days a week. They demanded a high level of mutual accountability: if anyone failed to arrive at the docks on time, it earned her an immediate phone call and a day or two of bad favor with other members of the team. Such commitment and accountability, of course, did not always result in perfect harmony; more often than not, they yielded only choppy water, painful blisters, grumbling, and a hodgepodge of pulls, tugs, and slides that was *anything* but harmonious.

Still, we had all committed ourselves to this crew. When our alarm bells rang well before sunrise, we did whatever was necessary to assemble our team on time and on the docks. We tried our best to keep our goal firmly in view, focusing upon the harmony that lay just around the corner . . . along with the medal that we hoped, if everyone paid careful attention and the conditions were just right, such harmony might eventually bring us. Not to any one of us would such a medal come, but to *all* of us, always as a team.

My two and a half years as a member of a crew team represent a watershed moment in my life and self-image, definitely the first and probably the last time I will ever recognize myself as anything like a real athlete. But these years also, I believe, offer some insight into one of Shankara's most compelling images for spiritual pursuit: the raft or boat of knowledge. Consider the following summary account of such pursuit and its desired results from one of the verse chapters of *A Thousand Teachings:*

> The seeker after truth should withdraw into the self the love for external things. For this love, secondary to that of the self, is inconstant and entails pain. [This seeker] should then take refuge in a teacher, a knower of *brahman* who is tranquil, free, bereft of actions, and established in *brahman,* as [the scriptures] say, "One who has a teacher knows" and "Know that."

> That teacher should immediately take the student . . . in the boat of the knowledge of *brahman* across the great ocean of darkness within.[13]

We catch a second, more fleeting glimpse of this raft in the concluding salutation of the same verse chapter: "[We] bow to the all-knowing teachers who have, by imparting knowledge, carried us across the great ocean of births and deaths, filled with ignorance."[14] The first passage dwells on a singular moment of recognition, belief, and trust, as treated in the previous two chapters. A seeker, filled with disgust and desire, takes refuge in a teacher, tranquil and securely established in the only true source and end of spiritual commitment. The second passage

[13] Shankara, *A Thousand Teachings,* Verse Portion 17.51-53, in Jagadananda, 206–7 (slightly modified).

[14] Ibid., Verse Portion 17.89, in Jagadananda, 217 (modified).

broadens this view to include other teachers, all those who have carried "us" across the ocean of ignorance. We bow, not just to our own teacher, but to our teacher's teacher, and even to *her* teacher—to all who have charted a course for us prior to our arrival on the docks.

These two passages offer an allusive, tantalizing portrait of what seems to be a powerful metaphor for *santati* or continuity of liberating truth. Like a boat or perhaps even like a rowing shell, this *santati* of seekers and teachers offers safe passage across ignorance to knowledge, across an ocean of bondage to the farther shore of freedom. We cannot make this crossing alone. We need a teacher inseparably joined to other teachers, a living link to those who have preceded us on the way.

On its own, Shankara's image of the raft would certainly attract my attention and invite reflection on how we might come to imagine and understand the phenomena of religious institutions more deeply. But, after years of studying Shankara and Augustine together, it is impossible for me to reflect on the raft of knowledge without also stealing a glance at an intriguingly comparable metaphor from *On Instructing the Uninstructed*:

> . . . by the symbol of the flood, wherein the just were saved by the wood [of Noah's ark], the Church to be was foreannounced, which Christ, her King and God, by the mystery of His Cross, has buoyed up above the flood in which the world is submerged . . . [Through this symbol, God] both gave a type of future judgment and foretold the deliverance of the just by the mystery of the wood.[15]

The idiom here is obviously quite different from that of our Hindu teacher, for Augustine is offering an allegorical reading of the Hebrew Torah to show its intrinsic coherence with the Christian revelation.[16] According to this interpretation, Noah's ark functions as a "type" or figure of the Christian community, wherein those elected to grace are

---

[15] Augustine of Hippo, *On Instructing the Uninstructed* 19.32, in Christopher, 62 (slightly modified).

[16] See Harmless, 126–30, 142–43; Marcel Dubois, "Jews, Judaism, and Israel in the Theology of Saint Augustine: How He Links the Jewish People and the Land of Zion," *Immanuel* 22/23 (1989) esp. 173–75, 186–201; Paula Fredriksen, "*Excaecati Occulta Justitia Dei:* Augustine on Jews and Judaism," *Journal of Early Christian Studies* 3 (1995) 313–16; and Paula Fredriksen, "*Secundum Carnem:* History and Israel in the Theology of St. Augustine," in *The Limits of Ancient Christianity: Essays on Late Antique Thought and Culture in Honor of R. A. Markus* (Ann Arbor: University of Michigan Press, 1999) 31–34.

carried across the waters of bondage by the wood of Jesus the Christ's death and resurrection. The ark, long a symbol of baptism in prior Christian tradition,[17] here emerges as a symbol of that into which new Christians are baptized, the spilling out or continuity of mutually indwelling love that defines the community from one generation to the next.

Together, Shankara's image of the raft and Augustine's symbol of the ark amplify our view of religious institutions like the Advaita teaching tradition or even the Christian Church. Such institutions are more like action verbs than substantive nouns; they represent something we do together rather than something that squats *out there* somewhere, apart from us.[18] At their best, they represent what might aptly be termed a *truly* ultimate team effort, a harmony of spiritual pursuit that aims for a permanence and fulfillment no medal could, in and of itself, ever provide. Like such a medal, this highest goal of human life will not come to any one of us alone. So, even if the hour may be inconvenient and our hands stinging from the blisters of yesterday's row, we drag ourselves out of bed, trudge down to the river bank, and present ourselves for training.

Receiving and Showing Promise

Images and metaphors are all very well. The continuity or spreading out of a perfect bond that joins an ideal teacher with similarly ideal students. A raft or ark to cross an ocean of ignorance and sin. The ultimate team effort for a truly ultimate goal. In and of themselves, these are beautiful images, and I am bold to believe that they genuinely enrich our visions of the religious institution, broadly defined.

Still, most of us are aware that not all teachers are ideal, and we may not be ideal seekers ourselves. God knows, I find myself doing almost *anything* to avoid prayer, reflection, or any of those other aspects of spiritual pursuit that put me face to face with my own tarnished self. And, although I participate consistently in the Church's worship, there are moments when it is not immediately obvious to me whether this is a

---

[17] See Jean Daniélou, S.J., *The Bible and the Liturgy* (Notre Dame, Ind.: University of Notre Dame Press, 1956) 75–85.

[18] See Joseph A. Komonchak, "The Epistemology of Reception," *The Jurist* 57 (1997) 187–94; and Michael J. Himes, "The Ecclesiological Significance of the Reception of Doctrine," *Heythrop Journal* 32 (1992) esp. 151–54.

gain or a loss. During the summer I spent writing this manuscript, for example, I trudged to various local churches as dutifully as ever I trudged to the banks of the Tennessee River, yet I recall precious few inspiring sermons or worship experiences that noticeably deepened my sense of clarity and commitment. Generally I was bored or, much to my chagrin, arrogantly disdainful of what I could not help but regard as ineptitude: insipid preaching, uninspiring or unintelligible prayer, almost unimaginably disinterested singing from the congregation. On a few occasions, I left the service angry and frustrated. If this summer were my only experience in the Church, I might have trouble believing that this raft is headed anywhere except to the bottom of the river.

Yet believe I *did* and *do,* and not merely because I knew that there were other parishes and more positive experiences of the Church, some as close to me as the beginning of the new academic year. By itself this fact would not have been enough to keep me trudging down the street to a local parish throughout the summer. There has to be more; in fact, I believe that there *is* more. Faced with teaching and worship that, in my considered if not unbiased judgment, falls short of the ideal, I do not feel particularly called to doubt that what happens in Church remains relevant both to my spiritual journey and to the journeys of those who join with me in our shared practice of faith. I am, instead, empowered and compelled by what I term, rather simply, "promise."

One side of this notion of promise is nicely revealed in the "Farewell Discourse" that appears at the beginning of the end of the Fourth Gospel (John 13-17). In this series of speeches given to the disciples immediately prior to Jesus' arrest, trial, and capital punishment at the hands of the political authorities of his day, the great teacher offers several images of Church that reinforce and deepen those we have already encountered. They include: a bond of mutual love and service symbolized by the disciples' washing of one another's feet (13:1-38); a vine whose member branches are joined directly to Jesus, the source of new life, when they bear good fruit (15:1-27); a learning community led together into ever greater truth and wisdom by the gift of the Spirit (16:1-15). These are beautiful images, to be sure, specifically designed to empower and compel the disciples as they navigate the traumatic events that are about to take place.

It is telling, however, that Jesus does not conclude this discourse with images or metaphors alone. He concludes, instead, with a prayer on the disciples' behalf:

> Sanctify [these disciples] in the truth; your word is truth. As
> you have sent me into the world, so I have sent them into the
> world. And for their sakes I sanctify myself, so that they also
> may be sanctified in truth.
>
> I ask not only on behalf of these, but also on behalf of those
> who will believe in me through their word, that they may all be
> one. As you, Father, are in me and I am in you, may they also be
> in us, so that the world may believe that you have sent me. The
> glory that you have given me I have given them, so that they
> may be one, as we are one, I in them and you in me, so that the
> world may know that you have sent me and have loved them
> even as you have loved me (John 17:17-23).

In this prayer we see, among other things, the beautiful imagery that
may be in the back of Augustine's mind when he suggests that teachers
and seekers come to dwell each in the other through shared sympathy
and a bond of love. Only here the stakes are considerably raised.
Through the disciples' sharing in the mission and sanctification proper
to himself, Jesus prays that they might come to participate, even as he
does, in the divine life of God. His wish for them is summed up in a
simple petition: Let them be one, as we are one.

This petition, however, also contains a promise. Jesus *asks* God for
sanctification, but he *declares* that he has already bestowed his own glory
upon his disciples, including both those seated before him and those
who will follow in their wake. His prayer on their behalf possesses a
kind of certainty and conviction that I personally feel only very rarely in
the midst of a petition for help. Jesus shows no real doubt that what he
asks of God will come to pass, and we are thus invited to do the same.

We can conclude that promise is, first, something that Christians
receive from that teacher par excellence, Jesus the Christ. It is a kind of
guarantee that our gathering together is not an accident or waste of
time, but is a partial, preliminary fulfillment of God's own desire to
gather us into the divine Self. So our hopes do not rest upon the bril-
liance of the individual preacher or the quality of an individual worship
experience in and of themselves. They rest upon a much more secure
foundation: a *promise,* freely offered by the source and end of our
spiritual striving.

At the same time, this does not exhaust the notion of promise. Indeed we encounter a very different side of this same promise from a

very different author writing about a very different moment in the scriptural narrative: that moment after Jesus of Nazareth's resurrection and ascension into heaven, when the disciples of Christ suddenly "come into their own" as a community of faith. The author of the two-volume work called "Luke-Acts" offers the following description of that special moment:

> All who believed were together and had all things in common; they would sell their possessions and goods and distribute the proceeds to all, as any had need. Day by day, as they spent much time together in the temple, they broke bread at home and ate their food with glad and generous hearts, praising God and having the goodwill of all the people (Acts 2:44-47a).

As subsequent events of the narrative will amply reveal, these new followers of Christ are not perfect. They will stumble, and fight, and disagree rather profoundly about the scope and purpose of their shared mission. But at this moment, so shortly after their master's suffering and glory, they show considerable promise as persons of faith and love. They break bread together, they care for the needy among them, they embody the twofold love of God and neighbor by praising God and earning the goodwill of those around them. They are not merely recipients of Jesus' promise. They are themselves *promising*, embodying God's desire for all humankind in their internal social order and their relationships with others.

Of course, both Jesus' prayer in the Fourth Gospel and the description of the early Christian community in Acts are—each in its own way—no less idealized than Shankara's description of the teacher in the previous chapter. Some historical critics have even suggested that such passages were crafted as much to confront perceived threats to the unity or vitality of their authors' respective communities as to reaffirm anything in their own experience.[19] Conflicts, inadequate teachers and

[19] For an overview of these visions as, in the terms of anthropologist Clifford Geertz, models *of* and models *for* community, see Reid Blackmer Locklin, "To Teach as the Evangelists Did? An Experiment in New Testament Theology," *Koinonia: The Princeton Theological Seminary Graduate Forum* 11/1 (1999) esp. 68–71. For more comprehensive treatments see, e.g., Raymond E. Brown, The *Community of the Beloved Disciple: The Life, Loves, and Hates of an Individual Church in New Testament Times* (New York/Mahwah: Paulist Press, 1979); Philip Francis Esler, *Community and Gospel in Luke-Acts: The Social and Political Motivation of Lukan Theology* (Cambridge: Cambridge University Press, 1987); Mark Allan Powell,

learners, and less than ideal circumstances no doubt pervaded their reality no less than they pervade ours. The point, then, is not that the communities of the New Testament period lived in perfect unity with God and harmony with one another, whereas contemporary communities do not. On the contrary. Very likely the authors of the Fourth Gospel and of Luke-Acts, no less than contemporary Christians, founded their commitment to the Church upon belief, trust . . . and also promise. They called their fellow Christians to remember God's promise in Christ and, at the same time, to strive mightily to see, develop, and reinforce the promise their institutions had, even if only tentatively around the edges, revealed within themselves. The single notion of promise thus becomes both consolation in the face of failure and a clarion call to do better in the future.

One constant temptation for the Church, and perhaps for other religious institutions as well, stems from a creeping tendency not to preserve both sides of this one promise. On the one hand, it is very easy to emphasize the promise given by God in Jesus the Christ to the exclusion of all else, so that we simply cease looking for promise in the institution and let it meander off unchecked into corruption or irrelevance. On the other hand, we can lapse into a kind of perfectionism that simply equates God's promise with the promise we glimpse or hope for in the religious institution. Then, when the institution or its members fall short of their own promise and expectations, as they invariably will, the institution must be rejected and left behind. And so we might find ourselves moving from community to community, from institution to institution, possibly even from religion to religion, looking for that perfect and seamless harmony that we have identified too bluntly with God's own promise and the perfect spiritual fulfillment contained therein.

As the reader might by now expect, I personally believe that the situation is rather more complicated and messy than either of these tendencies would seem to allow. Here again, I draw on my experience in crew. On the day my boat earned that first-place medal in Atlanta, for example, we did indeed show real promise. We started out strong and, more than once along the way, managed a near-perfect harmony of

---

What Are They Saying about Luke? (New York/Mahwah: Paulist Press, 1989) esp. 42–59; and David Rensberger, *Johannine Faith and Liberating Community* (Philadelphia: Westminster Press, 1988).

shared effort. As we closed on the finish, however, we were beginning to tire, and our only real competitor had veered so close to us that our oars were occasionally slapping against theirs. The final seconds of the race, as I remember them, were a confused pastiche of screaming from both boats, hopeless distraction, and more than a few cold splashes as our oars struck a discordant beat against the jagged surface of the river.

Our shell's bow did not cross the finish line first. Yet, because the other boat incurred a penalty for pushing us out of our lane, we won the race. The victory was neither tidy nor particularly stirring, but it was the first and only gold medal I ever received in an athletic contest.

I take a lesson from this experience, a lesson that helps me approach the occasional dry spells and inevitable disappointment we confront as participants in a religious institution. If we imagine the Church on the analogy of a boat, it is painfully obvious that seamless harmony is rarely evident in the lives of its members; more often than not, we are forced to confront dysfunction on both individual and corporate levels. Yet my one and only first-place medal suggests to me that appearances can indeed be deceptive. Receiving promise and showing promise belong together, but this does not guarantee that they will reveal themselves at precisely the same places and times. It's just possible that we may be approaching our goal precisely when we feel everything fall apart around us.

We walk a fine line when it comes to promise and the religious institution. Appearances *can* be deceptive, and so it becomes critically important not to celebrate success too quickly or to judge failure too harshly. We hold fast to what we believe, we call to mind what we remember, and we try our best to imagine what could be. And, most of all, we continue to show up.

New Family, New Birth

Believing, remembering, imagining, showing up—all of these pieces of the puzzle, essential to institutional commitment on the spiritual journey, also define another great institution that governs so much of our lives: the family.

For many of us, I suspect, the unique, ambivalent character of promise emerges very clearly with reference to our families. If there is anything the political leaders of the United States and of many other nations most consistently wrap in the rhetoric of promise, it is almost certainly the family. Healthy families are the key to healthy schools, we're told, in a popular if too simplified turn of phrase. Families are also the foundation of our way of life. When they fail or are placed "under siege" by various hobgoblins real or imagined, it is regarded as an assault upon society as a whole. God or Fate or simply the Fathers of our Country have promised us lives of wealth and stability, and this promise bears fruit in and through our families.

Even if the exalted political rhetoric that surrounds the family may arouse suspicion, it can hardly be doubted that many members of our societies do place great hope and trust upon it. And this hope does not seem entirely misplaced. Most families do show real promise, to one degree or another. Truly hellish and destructive exceptions regrettably abound. Nevertheless, it remains true that most of us approach our families with a general sense of gratitude and security, albeit a gratitude and security tempered by reserve. At moments, we may resent our parents or siblings, may feel embittered about hurts recent or long past, or may even wish to disentangle ourselves from complicated webs of favoritism, neglect, or obligation. But most of us will still turn to family supports when the need is great, and few would deny that who we are and who we become, for better or for worse, has everything to do with family.

Given the importance of family and its decisive role in forming us and giving shape to our lives, it seems natural enough that it also becomes yet another helpful point of entry for reconsidering the religious institution, both in its ideal aspects and even when it falls short of these ideals. In the Fourth Gospel Jesus speaks of spiritual rebirth through water and the Spirit (John 3:5), and the three so-called "Synoptic Gospels" each preserve a tradition in which he redefines his own family as "those who hear the word of God and do it" (Luke 8:21; cf. Mark 3:31-35; Matt 12:46-50). Preaching in his parish in Hippo on the "octave" of Easter—the eighth day after that great celebration of Christ's resurrection, the center and focus of the Church year, when new Christians were ordinarily baptized and received into the community—our Christian bishop draws both ideas together into a vivid depiction of the Church as institution and as mother:

> I am quite sure that it is no new or unheard of idea to you, but
> one very plain to your faith, that just as we were born in the
> flesh to our human parents, so too we are born in the spirit to

God our Father and the Church our mother. But of course it's the same Lord God who creates us from those natural parents of ours, and who recreates us from himself and the Church. In that birth we drag with us the chain of sin; in this one we have it broken. There, we are born in order to succeed parents who are going to die; here, to stay close to parents who remain so forever.[20]

In this sermon, Augustine is referring primarily to the rites of Christian initiation, including baptism, confirmation, and First Communion in the bread and wine of the Lord's Supper, and so his words cannot be entirely reduced to the bond of love and learning that joins teachers and seekers together on the spiritual journey. Yet, for Augustine and for Christian tradition generally, baptism is symbol and sacrament of the entire transformation of life effected by belief and trust, commitment and conviction.[21] This transformation, Augustine suggests, is like a new, eternal birth; through it, we find ourselves in a new spiritual family whose mother is none other than the institution itself. We find ourselves born anew, not merely in and through some isolated, mechanical ritual act, but also in and through those gathered to celebrate such rites and rituals . . . and, with them, all those who have been or ever will be similarly reborn.[22]

This idea, by itself, gives us ample food for thought. But, just as I could not treat Shankara's image of the raft without stealing a glance at Augustine and the symbol of the ark earlier in this chapter, so also here I cannot help but steal a glance at our Hindu teacher's own ideas about family and spiritual rebirth. Such ideas are already implicit in the very notion of *santati* as the continuity or spreading out of the Advaitin teaching tradition; indeed, one possible cluster of translations for *santati* includes "race," "lineage," and even "family."[23] The Upanishads

---

[20] Augustine of Hippo, *Sermon* 260C.1, in Edmund Hill, O.P., trans., *Saint Augustine: Sermons, The Works of Saint Augustine: A Translation for the 21st Century III/7*, ed. John E. Rotelle, O.S.A. (New Rochelle, N.Y.: New City Press, 1993) 194. The image of Church as mother was not new, of course, but had deep roots in prior tradition. See Joseph C. Plumpe, *Mater Ecclesia: An Inquiry into the Concept of the Church as Mother in Early Christianity* (Washington, D.C.: The Catholic University of America Press, 1943).

[21] Cf. Bernhard Lohse, *A Short History of Christian Doctrine: From the First Century to the Present*, rev. ed., trans. F. Ernest Stoeffler (Philadelphia: Fortress Press, 1985) esp. 136–41.

[22] See Augustine of Hippo, *Eighty-Three Different Questions* 59.4 and 75.2, in Mosher, 114–15, 192–93.

[23] Apte, 1618.

also, in several places, depict ways in which the teaching of truth can create new relationships even as it dissolves old ones, to bring even hardened enemies together as fellow travelers on the same path.[24]

Perhaps most strikingly, at one critical point in his commentary on the Prashna Upanishad, Shankara draws together many of these threads in terms no less vivid and forceful than those employed by Augustine. Commenting on the final verse of this Upanishad, in which a number of disciples together offer salutations to their teacher, Shankara expands considerably upon their words of praise:

> You are indeed our father, for you have, by [imparting] knowledge, generated for us a [new] body in *brahman*, which is eternal, undecaying, deathless and fearless. You alone have guided us by means of the raft of knowledge to the other shore of the ocean of ignorance [and] false knowledge, infested, as though [with] marine animals, with miseries such as birth, old age, death, illness and grief—[this is] called liberation, from which there is no return. Therefore, your fatherhood toward us is more fitting than that of the others [i.e., our natural parents]. The other father generates merely a physical body, yet he is most revered in the world. What then shall we say about the one who leads us to absolute fearlessness?[25]

Now, what exactly Shankara might mean by *brahma-sharira*, translated above as the new "body of *brahman*" bestowed by the teacher, remains a bit of a mystery, at least to me; to my admittedly limited knowledge, the term does not occur elsewhere in his writings. At a minimum, however, we might see behind the term a transformation no less profound than that symbolized and made effective by baptism in Augustine's North African parish, a complete refiguring of old relations and old priorities in light of new ones.[26] Thus it seems no less fitting for Shankara to

[24] See, e.g., the dialogues between Yajnavalkya and his wife Maitreyi in the Brhadaranyaka Upanishad 2.4 and 4.5, as well the episode in which the god Indra and the demon Virocana together seek instruction from Prajapati in Chandogya Upanishad 8.7-12. These are available in Olivelle, *Upanisads*, 28–30, 69–71, 171–75.

[25] For the Sanskrit text, see Panoli, vol. 2, 104. The translation in this case is my own, although I have consulted both Panoli and Swami Gambhirananda, trans., *Eight Upanisads, With the Commentary of Sankaracarya*, vol. 2 (Calcutta: Advaita Ashrama, 1992) 502–3.

[26] See Sengaku Mayeda, "Adi Sankaracarya's Teaching on the Means to Moksa: Jnana and Karman," *Journal of Oriental Research* 34/35 (1966) 73–75.

describe this transformation and the relationships predicated upon it under the analogy of a new, eternal birth and a new spiritual family generated through its continual reenactment from one generation to the next.

Before we pronounce that Augustine and Shankara are "doing basically the same thing" in these two passages, however, we should pause to take note of important differences between them. For we see that, in addition to significant doctrinal differences on such rather central issues as the person and work of Jesus the Christ (absent in Shankara) or the ultimate and absolute nondifference of self and God (disputed by Augustine),[27] they also speak about this new, spiritual family in slightly different ways. For Shankara, the individual teacher is described as "father" in his skillful employment of the raft of knowledge to bring seekers to the farther shore, and the family thus generated appears simply as *result* of this spiritual journey and its accompanying transformation. For our Christian bishop, although he ultimately ascribes the whole process to divine agency and will elsewhere speak of God the divine Self using strongly maternal language,[28] the "mother" and proximate agent of new birth is the Church, the religious institution itself. In Augustine's account, new family thus seems to emerge as a privileged *instrument* of transformation, rather than merely its result.

Of course, this apparent point of conflict softens quite a bit if we consider the analogy itself. Family begets family, not merely in the biological sense, but also in the sense that we acquire—again, for better or for worse—many of our most basic assumptions *about* family directly from the family or families that produced and shaped us. Perhaps gladly and deliberately, perhaps unconsciously, or perhaps despite our best efforts to the contrary, we inevitably find ourselves repeating habitual patterns of behavior or maintaining family traditions inherited from

---

[27] Although many of Augustine's statements not infrequently resemble those that might be made by Shankara, especially concerning the relation of God and world and the interior illumination of the mind by God, his doctrine of sin and grace, his personalistic conception of God, and even his Neoplatonic foundations probably render him much closer to that great rival of Shankara's "nondualism" *(advaita),* the "qualified nondualism" *(vishishtadvaita)* propounded especially by another great Hindu teacher and commentator named Ramanuja (1017–1137). Cf. Wilhelm Halbfass, ed., *Philology and Confrontation: Paul Hacker on Traditional and Modern Vedanta* (Albany: State University of New York Press, 1995) esp. 177–226.

[28] For a survey of such language, see Robert J. O'Connell, *Soundings in Augustine's Imagination* (New York: Fordham University Press, 1994) esp. 112–39.

our forebears. Naturally, there is always room for growth and change, along with the real possibility of failure and decline. We are never entirely divested of responsibility and free will in shaping our own lives and relationships. But if we ourselves show promise, however falteringly, as good sisters or brothers, wives, husbands, or partners, children or parents it is probably because we have observed such promise before, in those who preceded and surrounded us as we grew into adulthood. And if we have trust in the greater promise and gift of grace that such relationships could or should represent in our own lives, we are probably not the first in our families to do so. Family indeed begets family, in the most important and concrete senses of that word.

If this principle holds true for our natural or adoptive families of origin, then it seems particularly suitable for our new family of seekers and teachers, joined together in a shared effort of spiritual pursuit. In the words of that early English historian, the Venerable Bede, "Every day the Church gives birth to the Church."[29] We might further generalize this assertion, with Shankara's Advaita *sampradaya* or teaching tradition in mind: every day the institution gives birth to the institution, continually generating a spiritual family that is also itself the raft to reach the farther shore.

A Shared Communion

In the previous chapter, we used the analogies of friendship and fluency to explore the natural, almost spontaneous trust that joins seekers to teachers on the spiritual journey. Now, in light of the examples we have encountered in this chapter, we can note that, even if friendship and fluency may take their start from a relationship between two isolated individuals, they very rarely end there. One friendship leads to another, and, if we are true to ourselves and to one another, the bond of friendship deepens even as our circle widens to include still others who share our interests, our passions, and eventually much of our personal histories as well. As we acquire fluency in the language imparted by our teacher, we encounter whole new vistas of culture, society, and imagination. At some point, the terms "friendship" and "fluency" by themselves are no longer accurate. They fall short of describing the transformations

---

[29] Cited in Komonchak, "Epistemology of Reception," 193.

that have taken place, the new horizons that now shape our shared vision of the world, and even of ourselves. For this we need more profound analogies: mutually indwelling love, seamless continuity, new family, a perfect or even less than perfect harmony of hearts and minds—chanting together, breaking bread together, teaching and learning together, all of us joined inextricably to one another as we move up the slide, drop our oars into the water, and *pull*.

In the Christian tradition, especially in recent times, we might also find ourselves speaking in terms of what is sometimes called "the ecclesiology of communion."

At this point, we need to pause for a moment to sink our roots a bit more deeply into the theology and history of Catholic Christianity, particularly as this theology and this history were brought dramatically into focus between 1962 and 1965. During these years, Catholic bishops from throughout the world gathered in Rome to discuss and debate the most critical issues facing the Church. This series of meetings, entitled the "Second Vatican Council" or simply "Vatican II," dramatically changed the face of the Church. And these changes were, in turn, motivated and carried forward by two important ideals, one expressed by the Italian word *aggiornamento*, loosely translated as "modernization" or "updating," and the other by a French word, *ressourcement* or "returning to the sources." Pope John XXIII, who convened the council, desired that the Church should examine itself anew, to re-imagine its teachings and practices so as more effectively to speak a word of authentic hope and freedom to the modern world.[30] At the same time, the bishops and theologians of the council engaged this task, not merely through dialogue with the modern world and with each other, but also by returning once again to the essential vision of the Christian Scriptures, along with the writings of Augustine and other witnesses from the early centuries of the Church. The Second Vatican Council looked behind to look ahead, drawing on the wisdom of the past to address the challenges of present and future.

One tangible product of this shared effort was a truly impressive array of sixteen Church documents touching on a variety of issues, from

---

[30] See Dennis M. Doyle, *The Church Emerging from Vatican II*, rev. ed. (Mystic, Conn.: Twenty-Third Publications, 2002) 12–14; Hans Küng, *The Catholic Church: A Short History*, trans. John Bowden (New York: Modern Library, 2001, 2003) 181–87; and Avery Dulles, s.j., *The Reshaping of Catholicism: Current Challenges in the Theology of Church* (San Francisco: Harper & Row, 1988) 20–21.

liturgy and worship to the functioning and maintenance of parochial schools, from the legitimate freedom and diversity of religious expression to the religious foundations of a just economic and political order.[31] The scope of these documents is dizzying, even for many theologians. It's hard to imagine anyone trying to gather all these squirming puppies into one basket, to draw this mass of documentation together under any single basic notion or idea.

Yet this is precisely what happened in 1985. Twenty years after the conclusion of the council, again in Rome and again under the guidance of the Pope (albeit this time the Pope in question was John Paul II), a much smaller group of bishops from throughout the world again reflected anew, this time on the Second Vatican Council itself and its continuing impact upon the Church. This Extraordinary Synod of Bishops, as it was called, judged that there was one fundamental insight behind all those documents, an insight related to the council's "ecclesiology" or vision of the *ecclesia,* the Church. This vision, they suggested, can be summed up in one word: "communion."[32]

But what is "communion," and how does it relate to the institutional Church? Well, we can begin to answer this question by looking at how the bishops of the Synod tried to answer it. One passage from their final report offers a concise definition:

> What does the complex word *communion* mean? Fundamentally it is a matter of communion with God through Jesus Christ in the sacraments. Baptism is the door and the foundation of communion in the church. The eucharist is the source and the culmination of the whole Christian life (cf. *Lumen Gentium* [Vatican II's Dogmatic Constitution on the Church] 11). The communion of the eucharistic body of Christ signifies and produces, that is, builds up, the intimate communion of all the faithful in the body of Christ which is the church (1 Cor 10:16).[33]

---

[31] For overviews of the documents and of the fundamental vision of the council, see Doyle, *Church Emerging from Vatican II,* 16–24, and passim; Walter Kasper, "The Church as Communion: Reflections on the Guiding Ecclesiological Idea of the Second Vatican Council," in *Theology and Church* (New York: Crossroad Publishing Company, 1989) 148–65; and Francis A. Sullivan, s.j., *The Church We Believe In: One, Holy, Catholic and Apostolic* (New York/Mahwah: Paulist Press, 1988).

[32] 1985 Extraordinary Synod of Bishops, "Final Report," *Origins* 15 (December 19, 1985) 448.

[33] Ibid.

This short formula resonates with many other passages we have en-countered in this chapter, particularly Augustine's sermon on the octave of Easter and Jesus' petition and promise in the final moments before his arrest: Let them be one, as we are one. Such oneness is realized in a preliminary yet privileged way through Eucharist, also known as the Lord's Supper or just "Communion": a ritual thanksgiving and breaking of bread that, according to the tradition of the Church, is a true sharing in that "something more" that has defined our seeking from the very beginning, the divine source and end of our spiritual pursuit. Like bap-tism, however, such eucharistic sharing or Communion in bread and wine—the Body and Blood of Christ—cannot be divorced from the broader sharing or communion that is the religious institution itself. The Body of Christ that Christians receive in the eucharistic bread symbolizes and effects the spiritual body that we both believe we already are and strive ever more fully to become.

To be sure, the synod's formula represents a distinctively Catholic and sacramental vision of Christian communion, in which this com-munion is closely identified with the Eucharist that lies at the center of the Catholic Mass. Yet one of the great virtues of the notion "commun-ion" itself is the way that it can gather together many different facets and faces of the broader Christian movement.[34] In fact, theologian Susan Wood has highlighted the value of communion ecclesiology in bringing Christians from different denominations together to speak about the Church. Unlike so many other ways of addressing this topic, communion ecclesiology "defines the church in terms of those elements of faith and grace that create community rather than ecclesiastical structures" and, hence, "allows for degrees of unity among the various churches."[35] Empirically, communion comes to visible expression as a local community gathers in one place and time to embody shared values

[34] See especially Dennis M. Doyle, *Communion Ecclesiology: Vision and Versions* (Mary-knoll: Orbis Books, 2000); and Killian McDonnell, "Vatican II (1962–1964), Puebla (1979), Synod (1985): *Koinonia/Communio* as an Integral Ecclesiology," *Journal of Ecumenical Studies* 25 (1988) 399–427.

[35] Susan Wood, S.C.L., "The Theology of Communion as an Ecumenical Resource," in *Walking Together: Roman Catholics and Ecumenism Twenty-Five Years after Vatican II,* ed. Thaddeus D. Horgan (Grand Rapids, Mich.: William B. Eerdmans Publishing Company, 1990) 103. Cf. Susan Wood, S.C.L., "Ecclesial *Koinonia* in Ecumenical Dialogues," *One in Christ* 30 (1994) 124–45; Susan K. Wood, "Baptism and the Foundations of Communion," in *Baptism and the Unity of the Church,* ed. Michael Root and Risto Saarinen (Grand Rapids, Mich. and Cambridge, Mass.: William B. Eerdmans Publishing Company, 1998) 37–60.

and to engage in a fair variety of shared practices, including, but not reducible to, the breaking of bread in the Eucharist.[36] Historically, it also came to refer to letters of mutual recognition and other symbolic bonds that joined Christian bishops and their communities each to the other as, not merely individual, isolated churches, but indeed *the* universal Church of Christ.[37]

Finally, and perhaps most importantly, communion ecclesiology is rooted in a less tangible but no less real spiritual communion that defines both local communities and the institution as a whole: "The fundamental meaning of *koinonia* at the level of these invisible elements of communion is participation in the life of God in grace. . . . It fundamentally means 'sharing in one reality held in common.'"[38] Such sharing defines spiritual pursuit, of course, but it also defines the religious institution. At its most basic level, the Church *is* just such a "sharing in one reality held in common," a communion in that spiritual grace and divine reality inseparably joined to the institution itself.

Now, "sharing" is not quite the same thing as "oneness," although the two are closely related. Sharing implies common activity or effort, as well as a common spiritual fulfillment toward which alone such activity and effort are properly directed. Sharing can be done well, or it can be done badly. It also implies a kind of dynamism not unlike Shankara's term *santati:* a spilling over or spreading out, whereby the teaching and transformed life it provides are shared across space and time, seeker by seeker, teacher by teacher, community by community. Communion gives birth to communion precisely by *being* a communion—a crossroads of spiritual journeys and sharing in spiritual pursuit. It may take its start from that thoroughly ordinary yet mysterious moment of recognition that passes between a seeker and the teacher inexplicably well-suited to her deepest questions and confusions, but it certainly does not end there.

Indeed, if either our Christian bishop or our Hindu teacher is to be believed, true spiritual communion may not end at all . . . and this, in turn, leads us inexorably back to the Bala Vidya Mandir.

---

[36] Joseph Komonchak, "The Church Universal as the Communion of Local Churches," in *Where Does the Church Stand?* ed. Giuseppe Alberigo, Gustavo Gutiérrez, and Marcus Lefébure [Eng. lang. ed.], Concilium 146 (Edinburgh and New York: T & T Clark, Ltd. and the Seabury Press, 1981) esp. 31–32.

[37] See Sullivan, *Church We Believe In,* 34–65.

[38] Wood, "Ecclesial *Koinonia*," 128.

An Oar Stroke Closer to the Farther Shore

We began this chapter with brief snapshots of religious institution. A gathering of disciples in an elementary school gymnasium of Gandhi Nagar. A holder of the Shankaracharya office, surrounded by pilgrims in the Western Ghats. An assortment of devotees from all ethnic groups and all walks of life, chanting from prayer cards in a small New England chapel.

To this list we might now add others. A gathering of the earliest Christian disciples in and around the temple in Jerusalem. A Catholic bishop, surrounded by new initiates and other worshipers in the North African city of Hippo. An assortment of such bishops from throughout the world, assembling together in Rome from 1962 to 1965 to sort out some of the most critical issues of the Church. Perhaps even a campus ministry in Chattanooga, Tennessee, or a local parish in central Connecticut. Seekers and teachers, teachers and seekers, intertwined together as they chant, worship, break bread, debate, sing, roll out their mats, plant themselves, and get down to the serious, perilous business of teaching and learning and coming to share in that "something more" toward which all our lives are ultimately directed.

They may engage this shared effort well, or they may do so badly. Most likely, they fall out somewhere in between. But what draws these women and men together more than anything else, Hindu and Christian alike, is their shared conviction that their chanting and worshiping, teaching and learning are never a waste of time. In and through such sharing, the religious institution springs continually into existence. At its best, as we have seen, this institution can be viewed as a communion with the source and end of our spiritual pursuit—as a new, ongoing, and eternal birth. By sharing together in this way, participants trust that they are inching an oar stroke closer to the father shore.

This still leaves many questions unanswered, of course. Above all, there is the precise status of such religious institutions, including the Christian Church and the Hindu *sampradaya* of Advaita Vedanta, relative to one another. Even if both are viewed as rafts to carry seekers across an ocean of bondage, this does not by itself guarantee that both rafts are headed for the same shore. Both take shape in and through a sharing of belief and trust, recognition and commitment. But beliefs may conflict, and Christians and Hindus may or may not recognize themselves in one another. If we attempt to get behind the various truisms about tolerance or pluralism whose genuine value is exceeded only by their superficiality—one popular bumper sticker encourages us to "celebrate diversity," pure and simple, without effort or explanation—we will invariably find ourselves in the presence of sharply different claims and competing commitments: "My karma ran over your dogma," or conversely. At the end of the day, it just may not be possible for *everything* to be equally true or equally valid as we make our ways down the paths that have been set before us.

This issue was raised for me every single time those Sanskrit syllables began rolling out of the gathered disciples. Sitting there on the mats, fans turning ineffectually above my head, a Christian among Hindus, I was faced with a choice: should I join the chant? Usually I didn't, but this was not a very principled decision. At least half of the time, I couldn't figure out what we were chanting. Even when I did manage to piece this together, I was constrained by my rudimentary Sanskrit skills. Keeping up with the chant often required more concentration than I could reasonably manage on a Saturday or Sunday evening.

Sometimes, however, I was more deliberate. I always, *always* joined the Guru in the short invocations that immediately preceded and concluded instruction. These chants felt comfortable, even familiar. I never doubted that we were together invoking the same God and asking for blessings on an endeavor that we truly shared with one another. When I attended a ritual recitation of the thousand names of Lord Vishnu on New Year's Day, on the other hand, it did not take long for me to discern that I should not join the chant. It would, in my mind, have betrayed both my own Christian commitment and my respect for those around me to bless the offerings being made to an image of Vishnu by the recitation of a litany of sacred names and titles, some of which I no doubt would have preferred to apply to Jesus the Christ. So I sat in the midst of this profound spiritual family, recognizable *as* a family but also clearly different from my own, as they chanted, worshiped, and revealed a shared communion that I also could not call my own.

The Professor started me on my journey, and I had subsequently encountered first the Priest and then, about a decade later, the Guru. Both had transformed my vision of the religious institution. Both had opened doors to greater understanding and spiritual riches. But both also, precisely by transforming my vision and opening these doors, pressed the question of their mutual relation. To add still further layers to the issue, I could turn to the innumerable other priests and other gurus and other teachers of all different types and titles, from a wide spectrum of religious traditions and institutions. How do we make sense of our commitment to one in the light of so many? And then how do we understand these others we continue encounter along the way?

For these questions, we need still further wisdom. In my personal judgment we could do no better than to turn to the gentle instruction and sterling example of the Guide.

Chapter 4

On the Mystery of Others

The Guide

Earlier, I narrated my first interview with the Priest, a moment of clarity that eventually resulted in my baptism, confirmation, and First Communion in the Roman Catholic Church. Of course, that single moment, insightful and decisive though in many ways it was, did not settle the matter of my commitment all by itself. This process of discernment and preparation actually took the better part of two or three years, both before and after that critical interview, and it involved a fair variety of significant players. As I reflect back upon this period of my life, moreover, it is remarkable to me how few of those who influenced my decision to join myself to the Church were themselves Catholic.

There were my family and friends, for starters, who held various personal creeds and commitments, relatively few of them overtly religious. There was my girlfriend, an extraordinary woman who had made her own journey to the United Methodist Church some years before. Unless I am mistaken, the Professor was also Methodist. One of my closest friends and mentors, the assistant director of the student union where I worked weekends and evenings, eventually came to identify himself as an Episcopalian. There were also other influential members of the university faculty: a professor of English who was a former Baptist minister turned skeptic; an admired teacher and writer of literary fiction, whose attitude toward life seemed to have been decisively shaped by his years as a rescue helicopter pilot in Vietnam; the director of our University Honors program, who helped me frame and articulate much of what I was slowly coming to believe; and especially a professor of psychology whose considerable enthusiasm for my decision to convert to Catholicism puzzled and delighted me. Although I presume I will never know for sure, I strongly suspect that he might have been a fairly resolute atheist himself.

And then there was the Guide, who has consistently defied all of my attempts at classification.

I first encountered the Guide through a required course in music appreciation and music theory, yet what I discovered I was learning from her was, above all, an appreciation for philosophy and a substantial dose of feminist theory. Eventually, that single dose of feminist thought was no longer enough: during the semester of my baptism, I was one of several men enrolled in the Guide's class devoted exclusively to the topic. My preparation for reception into the Church and my studies in feminism and feminist theory seemed, at least in my mind, to cohere as harmoniously as the members of my rowing crew at their best. Both raised my heart and mind to a higher, more insightful, and also more critical and compelling view of the world and the role I might play in it. Both, I judged, brought me closer to the farther shore of my intellectual and spiritual pursuit.

Although this instinct about the ultimate coherence of what was drawing me to the Church and what was attracting me to feminist thought remains with me to this day, the largely unreflective confidence behind it has long since evaporated.[1] As it turns out, one of the greatest gifts the Guide offered to me—in another personal interview with a spiritual teacher in yet another office—was her willingness to interrupt my path for a spell, to contradict my naive assumptions about what commitments and beliefs can or cannot share the same space comfortably and without contradiction.

I can't remember for sure who initiated that particular meeting. But I recall the day as a warm one, a bright afternoon in early spring, with the sun still high in the sky and the bulky shadow of one of the campus's few free-standing sculptures against the brick face of the fine arts building. I went in the back entrance, climbed the steps, and tapped lightly on the Guide's office door.

---

[1] Cf. Denise Lardner Carmody, *The Double Cross: Ordination, Abortion, and Catholic Feminism* (New York: Crossroad Press, 1986).

In and of itself, the Guide's office scarcely resembled the Priest's neat, comfortable study in the Catholic student center or the dramatic simplicity of the Guru's Spartan apartment. It had all the marks of institutional design: long, narrow, and a bit on the dim side. Perhaps originally it had been designed with some other purpose in mind. Now it was lined with steel shelves practically bursting with books and sheets of music and other, more idiosyncratic decorations that I'm sure I have long since forgotten. I have a very vague, possibly even imagined, memory of a poster that depicted a hefty woman stuffing a skinny man completely into her vagina. It was definitely the office of a college professor.

Nevertheless, whether I knew it or not, I had come seeking spiritual instruction. And spiritual instruction is exactly what I got.

Within a few minutes of knocking on the office door, I found myself talking, or perhaps the word is *effusing*, about my imminent baptism in the Church. The Guide listened attentively and without surprise; most of what I was talking about had already come up more than once in class journals. At the same time, she began to raise questions and introduce a few observations of her own. What about the words of the apostle Paul about women keeping silent in Church? What about the texts of the early Fathers and Doctors of the Church—including even Augustine!—who so persistently taught that women should be subordinate to men? What about the continued insistence of the Roman Catholic institution that women should remain excluded from ordination, from most positions of leadership, and even in some cases from any consultation on issues that directly affect their lives? If I had any commitment at all to a feminist reading of social structures, shouldn't these uncomfortable realities significantly challenge my ability to commit myself to the Church? Question after question, issue after issue, the Guide pressed me to clarify. Finally, she paused, looked me in the eye, and gently offered some rather tough words: "You wouldn't even consider joining the Ku Klux Klan, would you? Then how can you agree to be baptized in the Catholic Church?"

The one thing I remember most clearly about this moment, and the conversation as a whole, is that I never felt the least bit threatened or attacked. The Guide's very presence invited freedom and trust. At the beginning and end of the conversation, moreover, she carefully placed her criticism in a broader context by paraphrasing the great comparative mythologist Joseph Campbell: "You really do have to follow your own bliss." She wasn't trying to stop me from making a commitment to the Church. She *was* forcing me to defend this decision in the light of other, possibly conflicting claims that she knew full well I was also trying to make my own. And so I thought about her questions and offered various explanations, most of which amounted to a judgment that the forces of liberation have deeper roots in the Church's history and theology—again, including even Augustine!—than do the forces of oppression. That this fact is not always evident in the Church's institutional structures could not, in my mind, dislodge the more positive overall judgment.

I don't think my arguments convinced the Guide. Later, after my baptism, confirmation, and First Communion, she would point out how the rites themselves revealed the inextricably patriarchal character of the religious institution. She liked the Priest, to be sure, and I think she particularly appreciated the way he seamlessly wove explicit rejections of racism and sexism into my baptismal promises. But she also pointed out that there was never a moment in the celebration in which he, precisely as a *he,* was not completely in charge. At least in this ritual context, it seemed, the Church was not rejecting the very structures of sexism and oppression I had been called to reject as a member of it. This could be a case of different roots, some deeper than others. Or it could just be good old-fashioned hypocrisy.

Observations like these revealed that the Guide was probably not moved by my arguments in favor of the Roman Catholic Church. But they also revealed something else, something as obvious as it was profound. They revealed that she was *there*. At the moment my decision actually brought me decisively into the Church, the Guide was among those gathered to celebrate the event. And, at that very moment and without any reluctance I could detect, the Guide did something that, like the recognition that joins seeker and teacher on the spiritual journey, was at one and the same time thoroughly ordinary and deeply mysterious.

The Guide offered a joyful smile and a warm embrace to welcome me home.

An Upset Balance?

With each passing year, I find myself reflecting more and more frequently about these two sides of the Guide, one offering a fairly harsh assessment of the institutional Church and the other welcoming me joyfully into its ranks. Part of it, of course, is just that she was an outstanding mentor and good friend: she possessed the personal maturity to rejoice in my ability to reach my own informed judgments, even if they were different from those she might choose for me. But I believe her attitude also flowed from a keen spiritual insight. Indeed, of all the persons I have ever known, it is she who has come most clearly to symbolize a deep, potentially fruitful tension that cuts right through the center of the closely related pursuits of spiritual communion and institutional commitment. Those very elements that define our spiritual journeys and our connections to religious institutions—belief and trust, conviction and commitment—necessarily include some measure of discernment, judgment, and even rejection. If our conviction has blossomed as knowledge, it would be untrue to ourselves and to the risks we have taken to pretend it is something other than an authentic disclosure of God, of the world, and of ourselves as seekers. At the same time, we will not infrequently encounter others whose convictions differ profoundly from our own, others who, through the very integrity of their claims and their lives, call forth at least some measure of respect, acceptance, and even joy. In the diverse communions of belief and commitment that define these others and their spiritual journeys, we may well recognize aspects of ourselves and our religious traditions. In the *content* of those beliefs and *intended goal* of those commitments, however, we may sharply disagree.

The wisdom of the Guide was to reveal by word and action that neither side of this tension need be ignored or set aside for the spiritual quest to be a true one. Rejection and acceptance, critique and welcome —both, I believe, are part and parcel of an appropriately balanced spirituality of institutional commitment. To emphasize one at the expense of the other runs the risk of betraying them both.

A rapid survey of the long history of actual religious institutions, however, readily suggests that this balance has too often been tipped in favor of rejecting others, of reserving our welcome and acceptance solely for those who share our own belief and trust. If we have judged that our own religious tradition represents a true communion in the source and end of spiritual pursuit, a harmony or spilling over of spiritual instruction that is simultaneously raft to carry seekers across an ocean of bondage and new, eternal birth for those who are thus carried —if we have come to view the institution as an authentic sign and instrument of liberation, of unity and union, of ultimate salvation[2]—then other teachings and institutions too easily emerge as competitors or detractors on the way. It is by no means clear that they are headed in the same direction as we are; perhaps we even fear some kind of collision on the high seas of our spiritual journeys. With such fears nagging at the backs of our minds, we live with a nearly constant temptation to opt for what might at first seem better, safer, truer to who we are and where we have placed our hope and trust. We reject, we exclude, we sink the other boats where they stand or, at least, keep ourselves and our cargos entirely clear of them and of the threat they may seem to represent.

In the Christian tradition, this response has recently and persuasively been given the label "exclusivism," and it is closely associated with a phrase first employed by the third-century Father of the Church, Cyprian of Carthage: "*Extra ecclesiam nulla salus*," "No salvation outside the Church."[3] As it happens, Cyprian himself never applied this axiom to non-Christians, but this has not prevented later Christians from doing just that.[4] Indeed, for all his breadth and wisdom on so many matters, our Christian bishop Augustine's views tend rather strongly toward exclusivism. In the Fourth Gospel, Jesus announces, "I am the way, and the truth, and the life. No one comes to the Father except through me" (John 14:6). Augustine for his part came ever more closely, particularly toward the end of his life of teaching and ministry, to

---

[2] This phrase deliberately echoes the language of Vatican II's Dogmatic Constitution on The Church. See *Lumen Gentium* 1, in Flannery, 1.

[3] See Diana L. Eck, *Encountering God: A Spiritual Journey from Bozeman to Banaras* (Boston: Beacon Press, 1993) 170–78; James L. Fredericks, *Faith among Faiths: Christian Theology and Non-Christian Religions* (New York/Mahwah: Paulist Press, 1999) 16–22; Paul F. Knitter, *No Other Name? A Critical Survey of Christian Attitudes Toward the World Religions*, American Society of Missiology Series 7 (Maryknoll, N.Y.: Orbis Books, 1985) 75–119; and Paul Knitter, *Introducing Theologies of Religions* (Maryknoll, N.Y.: Orbis Books, 2002) 19–50. Although questions can be raised about the adequacy of the triple pattern of "exclusivism," "inclusivism," and "pluralism" first introduced by Alan Race (in his 2002 survey, for example, Knitter prefers "replacement," "fulfillment," and "mutuality"), these terms enjoy wide recognition and amply serve the purposes of a short chapter such as this one. For brief overviews, see Eck, *Encountering God*, 168–69; and Fredericks, *Faith among Faiths*, 13–16.

[4] See the discussions in Gavin D'Costa, "'Extra Ecclesiam Nulla Salus' Revisited," in *Religious Pluralism and Unbelief: Studies Critical and Comparative* (London and New York: Routledge, 1990) 130–47; Jacques Dupuis, S.J., *Toward a Christian Theology of Religious Pluralism* (Maryknoll, N.Y.: Orbis Books, 1997) 86–96; and especially Francis A. Sullivan, S.J., *Salvation Outside the Church? Tracing the History of the Catholic Response* (New York/Mahwah: Paulist Press, 1992) 20–24.

equate such statements with explicit Christian profession and baptism in the Church. Even unbaptized infants and adults who have never heard the Gospel would, according to Augustine's interpretation, find themselves outside the saving grace of God.[5] Different gifts of conversion there may well be, as we saw in chapter 1. But, if the conversion is a true one, it will always be a conversion to Christ and will eventually lead the seeker into the bosom of the Church.

Our Hindu teacher's views are, on the whole, more complex. Both the general Hindu doctrine of reincarnation and Shankara's own distinctive teaching of *advaita* prevent him from suggesting that any human person can ever be conclusively separated from God or spiritual fulfillment. Nevertheless, such tolerance on a cosmic level does not prevent Shankara from using very colorful language to describe the devotees of other teaching traditions, here and now. Such persons are "only to be pitied," their traditions are flawed, and so they can be dismissed as "arch rogues and demoniacs," "persons of little intellect," and "those who are devoid of scriptural knowledge and the grace of the teacher."[6] To spiritual seekers, moreover, Shankara offers the following advice:

> The conceptions [of rival Hindu schools and of Buddhists] about bondage and liberation lack deep reflection. They should never be accepted, for they are not supported by reason and the scriptures. Hundreds and thousands of errors on their part could be mentioned.
>
> A wise person, having renounced the teachings of others' scriptural traditions and having discarded all crookedness, should with faith and devotion acquire a firm understanding of the true meaning of the Vedantas accepted by Vyasa.[7]

Here the balance is definitely tipped in the direction of critique. According to Shankara, the true seeker and person of wisdom is the one who looks at other teaching traditions and sees little or anything of real value. The result? Renunciation of other scriptures, rejection of those others themselves as mere obstacles on the path of knowledge.

[5] Sullivan, *Salvation Outside the Church?* 28–29.

[6] Shankara, Commentary on Brhadaranyaka Upanishad 2.1.20, in Panoli, vol. 4, 467–73 (slightly modified).

[7] Shankara, *A Thousand Teachings,* Verse Portion 16.64b-65 and 66b-67, in Jagadananda, 187–88 (modified).

At first glance, this may seem an exceedingly closed-minded view of reality, and in some ways it is. Yet neither Shankara nor Augustine can be easily dismissed. Their statements may well be unbalanced, but they still reveal profound insight into authentic spiritual striving and discernment. Not all beliefs are compatible, and not every conviction we encounter on the way will be true. What the views of these great teachers may lack in imagination, they more than make up for in pure, unflinching honesty. Augustine and Shankara, no less than the Guide, do not mince words when it comes to spiritual pursuit and institutional commitment. They call it like they see it.

This same insight, simple and obvious as it is, struck me rather suddenly during my time with the Guru. It was a normal winter morning in Chennai, which meant that my undershirt was drenched with sweat almost from the moment my foot made contact with the bicycle pedal. I had spent significant time in the past few days, not only preparing Shankara's *A Thousand Teachings* for our regular reading together, but also reviewing the final portions of Augustine's *Confessions*. Then, as I pedaled to the Guru's apartment, my mind started churning, my heart-rate increased, and I found myself racing to arrive as soon as I possibly could. Once there, I burst into his office, fumbled through our invocations, and nearly spat out the words: "We can't both be right!"

It had suddenly fallen together for me, in a way it never had when my only real contact with the Hindu tradition had been through books. The Guru was a real, living Hindu person, and an Advaitin to boot. He asserted with great confidence and clarity that liberation consists entirely in a firm knowledge of one's ultimate identity in and as God the divine Self. I was a Christian, who looked to the future for an eternal communion with a God distinct from myself, a God whom I also understood as Trinity, as unity-in-difference. Absolute identity was out of the question. The Guru and I might both be wrong, to one degree or another, but we absolutely *could not* both be right—at least, not from within any frame I could very easily imagine.

As I remember this exchange, the Guru wobbled his head in a distinctively Indian gesture of approval, offered another of his wide smiles, and replied, "Ahhhh, good. That's correct." Later in my studies, after I had told him more about Christian faith and practice, he would suggest that Christianity sounded a lot like Hindu teaching traditions of *bheda-abheda*, "difference and unity," or *vishishta-advaita*, "qualified non-difference." In effect this meant, even though the Guru was far too gracious ever to express it quite this way, that Christian doctrine sounded a lot like some erroneous views that Shankara and his followers had expended great time and energy to refute.

So there we were, facing each other, having agreed together that our beliefs were incompatible at a profound level, that we could not both be right about the ultimate source and end of all our strivings. Perhaps, had we followed the examples of Shankara and Augustine very rigidly, this conversation would have been the end of it. I would have packed up my bags and set off for home.

Instead, we opted for the example of the Guide. We smiled at one another, recovered our balance, and joyfully continued our shared study and conversation.

Stretching the Boundaries of Communion

Not too long ago, I attempted an experiment with one of my classes, an experiment that nicely reveals how deeply Christian exclusivism has shaped contemporary perceptions of the institutional Church. The class was entitled "Christian Faith in the Modern World," and the students came from a range of Christian denominations, as well as including many who would not identify themselves with any religious tradition at all. As the semester progressed and we delved into Christian doctrines of God, creation, and redemption, students began quite properly to ask about the uniqueness of Christ and Christian salvation. One day, having sifted through more than a few group reports that complained about Catholics in particular for their intolerance, I decided to test something. I simply walked into class and made a request: "If you believe that the Roman Catholic Church teaches that non-Catholics are absolutely wrong and damned to hell for eternity, please put up your hand."

Nearly every hand in the classroom went up. Of the approximately twenty-five students in the class, as many as twenty, including Catholics, Protestants, and skeptics alike, affirmed that the Church does indeed condemn all non-Catholics absolutely and without reservation. Needless to say, I was appalled.

At the same time, I was not entirely surprised. For I probably would have made the same assumption as a young undergraduate. Having grown up in northeast Georgia and then attending school in Chattanooga,

Tennessee—we used to call it the "Buckle of the Bible Belt," though I'm sure there are rival claimants to *that* title—I had run into my share of Bible-thumpers who spoke with great confidence and cheer about the impenetrable darkness and inevitable, unending torment of all those persons who do not profess Christ in the prescribed manner. These condemned persons, certainly including skeptics like myself and not infrequently (much to my amusement) also members of other Christian denominations, represented the work of the devil, pure and simple. When I first began attending Mass at the Catholic student center as an observer, I suppose I assumed that with Catholicism I would encounter basically the same line, except more so.

Weeks or months later, as I found myself becoming more and more attracted to the Catholic faith, I tried to use its presumed exclusivism as a possible way out. I made yet another appointment with the Priest and let him in on a little secret. "There's something I guess you should know. I could never become part of a tradition that automatically condemns all other religions as false and their followers as damned to hell. That doesn't make any sense to me."

"Good," he replied. "It doesn't make all that much sense to the Church, either." Then, after a bit more discussion, he passed along a short document for me to read at my leisure.

The reading in question was *Nostra Aetate,* the Vatican II Declaration on the Relation of the Church to Non-Christian Religions. One of the final documents to be produced by the bishops of the council, this declaration can be interpreted as restoring some kind of balance between acceptance and rejection, welcome and critique, in the communion of the Roman Catholic Church, as well as attempting to infuse joy and hope into its dealings with the followers of other religions. For Catholics, as well as not a few others, it opened a door to examine the relationship between the Church and other religions anew, to question whether the exclusivist answer is really the only authentically Christian response to religious pluralism and diversity.

In the sections that follow, we will consider some of the alternative proposals that have followed in the wake of the Second Vatican Council. But first, we should dwell a bit longer on *Nostra Aetate* itself. Since this document was so important for me in my discernment and so nicely captures what I believe was the essential insight of the Guide, I think it is worth quoting at some length here.

An introductory section sets out the basic vision of the council:

Humanity forms but one community. This is so because all stem from the one stock which God created to people the entire earth (see Acts 17:26), and also because all share a common destiny, namely God. His providence, evident goodness, and saving designs extend to all humankind (see Wis 8:1; Acts 14:17; Rom 2:6-7; 1 Tim 2:4) against the day when the elect are gathered together in the holy city which is illumined by the glory of God, and in whose splendor all peoples will walk (see Apoc 21:23 ff.).

People look to their different religions for an answer to the unsolved riddles of human existence. The problems that weigh heavily on people's hearts are the same today as in past ages. What is humanity? What is the meaning and purpose of life? What is upright behavior, and what is sinful? Where does suffering originate, and what end does it serve? How can genuine happiness be found? What happens at death? What is judgment? What reward follows death? And finally, what is the ultimate mystery, beyond human explanation, which embraces our entire existence, from which we take our origin and towards which we tend?[8]

This vision is truly *catholic,* or universal, in its scope. From the highest point of view, it sets outs God's design for all humankind, a saving will that reaches out to each and every human being. At the same time, the bishops of the council also presume a great deal of empirical consensus on those big questions of life and existence that motivate spiritual inquiry. Exploring similar questions and embraced by the same love of God, all humankind stands together as one community.

In the next section, the bishops touch briefly on the concrete diversity of actual religions, singling out Hinduism and Buddhism for special mention. The statement that follows this brief recognition is quite programmatic:

The Catholic Church rejects nothing of what is true and holy in these religions. It has a high regard for the manner of life and conduct, the precepts and doctrines which, although differing in many ways from its own teaching, nevertheless often reflect a ray of that truth which enlightens all men and women. Yet it proclaims and is in duty bound to proclaim without fail, Christ

---

[8] *Nostra Aetate* 1, in Flannery, 569–70.

who is the way, the truth and the life (Jn [14:6]). In him, in whom God reconciled all things to himself (see 2 Cor 5:18-19), people find the fullness of their religious life.

The church, therefore, urges its sons and daughters to enter with prudence and charity into discussion and collaboration with members of other religions. Let Christians, while witnessing to their own faith and way of life, acknowledge, preserve and encourage the spiritual and moral truths found among non-Christians, together with their social life and culture.[9]

Subsequent paragraphs of the document dwell in greater detail upon the Church's relationship with Islam and especially with Judaism, as well as condemning all forms of discrimination. But the basic principles are already in place. Without relinquishing their commitment to the decisive truth and fulfillment found in Jesus the Christ, the bishops of the council nonetheless call Christians not only to tolerate those who follow other religious paths, but even to "acknowledge, preserve and encourage the spiritual and moral truths" such persons and their traditions may well represent.

One of the aspects of this declaration that most impressed me as a young undergraduate was its length . . . or, more properly, its lack thereof. As compared with other documents of the council, which go on for pages and pages, a standard English translation of *Nostra Aetate* amounts to under twenty short paragraphs and takes only a few minutes to read. As a result, there is much that it does not say. It does not explicitly grant that the followers of other religious traditions are solidly within the realm of God's grace and salvation; for statements such as these, we must turn to *Lumen Gentium*, the Dogmatic Constitution on the Church.[10] Neither does *Nostra Aetate*, proper to its stated subject, extend this same grace beyond the boundaries of religion itself to include all persons of goodwill, including even the most resolute atheist; this conviction we encounter most clearly in *Gaudium et Spes*, the Pastoral Constitution on the Church in the Modern World.[11] Finally and most importantly, the bishop's declaration on the Church's relation to other religions does not address *how* what it describes is possible, that is, *how precisely* other religious traditions and their followers possess spiritual

---

[9] *Nostra Aetate* 2, in Flannery, 570–71.

[10] See *Lumen Gentium* 16, in Flannery, 21–22.

[11] See especially *Gaudium et Spes* 21–22, in Flannery, 183–87.

truths worth preserving and even encouraging when the teachings of these same traditions may well contradict those of the Church. *Ad Gentes*, the Decree on the Church's Missionary Activity, answers this question with great economy. It simply states that God reaches to non-Christians and brings them to a true, saving faith "in ways known to himself."[12]

All of these questions and issues go beyond what *Nostra Aetate*, in its attractive simplicity, appears content to accomplish. In this short document the bishops of the council simply offer a vision of a larger community or even communion, a vision that transcends the formal boundaries of the Church. This larger community may well find its highest meaning and complete fulfillment in and through a particular religious institution—namely, the Church—but it cannot be too strictly confined therein. Christians are thus called to establish close relations with other religious persons in confident expectation that they will encounter not only error but also truth, not only what is contradictory to the Gospel but also what is holy and sanctified by God. They are called, in short, to stretch the boundaries of their spiritual communion.[13]

This was and is an attractive idea for me. At the time I was considering joining the Church, moreover, I viewed it as a fairly distinctively Roman Catholic position. Having spent most of my life in what I regarded as an island of secular tolerance in the midst of a particularly exclusivist brand of evangelical Protestantism, I couldn't imagine most other Christians making such a broad and inclusive vision their own.

I was wrong. As circumstances would have it, at very close to the same moment that I encountered *Nostra Aetate* for the first time, an ecumenical group of Protestant, Orthodox, and Catholic scholars was working in Switzerland under the aegis of the World Council of Churches to stretch the boundaries still further. The "Baar Statement," which was the fruit of their labor, includes the following words:

> We see the plurality of religious traditions as both the result of the manifold ways in which God has related to peoples and nations as well as a manifestation of the richness and diversity of humankind. We affirm that God has been present in their seeking and finding, that where there is truth and wisdom in their

[12] *Ad Gentes* 7, in Flannery, 451.
[13] See Dupuis, *Toward a Christian Theology of Religious Pluralism*, 161–70; Knitter, *No Other Name?* 120–44; and Francis A. Sullivan, *The Church We Believe In: One, Holy, Catholic and Apostolic* (New York: Paulist Press, 1988) esp. 109–31.

teachings, and love and holiness in their living, this, like any
wisdom, insight, knowledge, understanding, love and holiness
that is found among us, is the gift of the Holy Spirit. . . .[14]

Harvard professor Diana Eck, herself a Christian with extensive experience in interreligious dialogue, rightly points out that this statement goes a bit beyond *Nostra Aetate*, identifying in the diversity of religious traditions not merely a "seeking" but also without reservation a "finding" of God.[15] The wisdom and holiness that may be found in various religious traditions, like *any* wisdom or holiness "that is found among us"—presumably *including* Christians and the Church—are regarded as a true gift of that "something more" all of us have been seeking, and perhaps even finding, in the tangled courses of our spiritual journeys. If so, then a relationship of shared dialogue and collaboration will, much like our shared participation in religious institutions themselves, never be a waste of time. Indeed, we may discover that such a relationship represents a next step on the spiritual journey, yet *another* oar stroke bringing us closer to a shore we had, up to that point, scarcely imagined.

The Beloved Outsider

At the conclusion of chapter 2 we observed how, once we have stumbled across the path of the right teacher, we may gradually or suddenly discover that we are not alone, that others have preceded and surround us on the way, that our sharing in spiritual instruction is intimately wrapped up in a broader sharing or communion that is the religious institution. In *Nostra Aetate* and the "Baar Statement" we encounter a similar moment in the lives of institutions themselves. They too may not be entirely alone, and they too may have something to gain from a sharing in spiritual insight and instruction.[16]

---

[14] Quoted in Eck, *Encountering God*, 188. She quotes from the full text of the "Baar Statement" in S. Wesley Ariarajah, "Theological Perspectives on Plurality," *Current Dialogue* (June 1990) 2–7.

[15] Eck, *Encountering God*, 188.

[16] Cf. Fredericks, *Faith among Faiths*, esp. 139–80; Francis X. Clooney, S.J., *Hindu God, Christian God: How Reason Helps Break Down the Boundaries between Religions* (Oxford: Oxford University Press, 2001); and Jacques Dupuis, S.J., *Christianity and the Religions: From Confrontation to Dialogue,* trans. Phillip Berryman (Maryknoll, N.Y.: Orbis Books, 2001).

But the account offered by *Nostra Aetate,* as we noted, is deliberately clipped and restrained. It points a way beyond exclusivism, but it falls short of charting a course to another harbor. If other religious traditions are not simply competitors or obstacles on the way, but are in some important sense fellow travelers, how does this change our understanding of Christian communion itself? What further imaginative leaps are required to close the gap between the Church's membership rosters and the universal spiritual community to which the opening paragraphs of *Nostra Aetate* seem to allude? On these issues the bishops of the council, perhaps wisely, generally held their tongues.

Many others have picked up where they left off. Among the most prominent of these, the German theologian Karl Rahner, himself an influential voice in shaping the text of *Nostra Aetate,* offered a kind of solution by making the followers of other religious traditions de facto members of the Christian communion:

> . . . somehow all men *[sic]* must be capable of being members of the Church; and this capacity must not be understood merely in the sense of an abstract and purely logical possibility, but as a real and historically concrete one.—But this means in its turn that there must be degrees of membership in the Church, not only in ascending order . . . but also in descending order from the explicitness of baptism into a non-official and anonymous Christianity which can and should yet be called Christianity in a meaningful sense, even though it cannot and would not describe itself as such.[17]

Such a position is often referred to as "inclusivism," because it intends to *include* the followers of other religions, and possibly also the religions themselves, within a considerably enlarged understanding of Christian doctrine and the Church. Those who were previously outsiders to the tradition are increasingly recognized as insiders . . . but the understanding of the tradition is not necessarily revised in light of these others' sudden and potentially awkward inclusion. The boundaries of

---

[17] Karl Rahner, "Anonymous Christians," in *Theological Investigations, Vol. VI: Concerning Vatican Council II,* trans. Karl-H. and Boniface Kruger (New York: Crossroad Publishing Company, 1982) 391. On the strengths and weaknesses of Rahner's inclusivism, see Dupuis, *Toward a Christian Theology of Religious Pluralism,* 143–49; Fredericks, *Faith among Faiths,* 24–33; Knitter, *Introducing Theologies of Religions,* 68–75; and Sullivan, *Salvation Outside the Church?* 162–81.

communion may be stretched, but the vision of communion itself has not substantively changed.

A second strategy turns this idea inside out, recommending that the Church simply recognize its place as one among many participants in a much wider spiritual and social reality. Thus in 1972—just seven years after the Second Vatican Council—the bishops of the newly formed Federation of Asian Bishops' Conferences boldly initiated a "triple dialogue" with the religions, cultures, and common people of their native lands. Although built upon inclusivist assumptions, this initiative took *Nostra Aetate* and even Karl Rahner a step further, envisioning the followers of other religions primarily as *collaborators* in a shared task of alleviating poverty and overturning unjust systems of oppression.[18] American theologian Paul Knitter has taken a similar tack, but with more far-reaching conclusions. Describing his proposal in terms of a shift from an "ecclesiocentric" or Church-centered view to one that is "soteriocentric" or centered upon spiritual and socioeconomic liberation, Knitter proposes that all religions and their institutions stand together as approximately equal partners in the struggle for justice. To the degree that they engage in this struggle well, they participate in an even more inclusive kind of shared communion, a shared striving for economic equity, just political structures, and indeed the very kingdom of God on earth.[19] Here, what might previously have been regarded as the firm boundaries of true spiritual communion are not just stretched, but broken. Communion itself has been redefined.

Diana Eck reflects many of the fundamental concerns of theorists like Paul Knitter and pastoral organizations like the Federation of Asian Bishops' Conferences when she speaks of a new "imagined community" and a "wider sense of 'we.'"[20] The point is not so much to envision others as insiders to our own community as to recognize a broader community to which all of us and our institutions can, to one

---

[18] See Thomas C. Fox, *Pentecost in Asia: A New Way of Being Church* (Maryknoll, N.Y.: Orbis Books, 2002) esp. 22–37. Cf. A. Alangaram, *Christ of the Asian Peoples: Towards an Asian Contextual Christology, Based on the Documents of the Federation of Asian Bishops' Conferences* (Bangalore: Asian Trading Company, 1999).

[19] See especially Paul F. Knitter, "Toward a Liberation Theology of Religions," in *The Myth of Christian Uniqueness: Toward a Pluralistic Theology of Religions,* ed. John Hick and Paul F. Knitter (Maryknoll, N.Y.: Orbis Books, 1987) 178–200; and Paul F. Knitter, *Jesus and the Other Names: Christian Mission and Global Responsibility* (Maryknoll, N.Y.: Orbis Books, 1996).

[20] See Eck, *Encountering God,* 200–31.

degree or another, claim insider status. This is a position that Eck, among others, labels "pluralism."

I have great personal sympathy for both inclusivist and pluralist accounts of the Church's relation to other religions and religious institutions. On a strictly intellectual plane, I tend to think mainly in inclusivist terms. When I tried to explain to the Guru why exactly I could never believe that he would be damned simply for being a Hindu, for example, I unfolded my explanation from distinctively Christian convictions about the all-encompassing grace of Jesus the Christ. On the other hand, when it comes to practical matters of dialogue and collaboration, I generally work from pluralist assumptions. It seems easiest and most productive to presume that my dialogue partners and myself are fellow travelers on a common journey, fellow participants in a common social and spiritual endeavor that transcends any of our particular religious traditions. With both tendencies in mind, one might say I see myself as something like a "theoretical inclusivist" and a "practical pluralist."[21]

In my spiritual life, however, I have increasingly found both inclusivism and pluralism inadequate to frame and guide my journey or, I am bold to believe, the journeys of many who preceded and surround me. Perhaps, given the complex tapestry of risk and commitment that joins us to our religious institutions in the first place, these two proposals seem just a little too clean and a little too easy. In the drive to view members of other religious traditions, or simply the members of *all* religious traditions, as fellow sharers in a communion we recognize as our own, something is surely gained. But something may also be lost.[22] Specifically, when I read inclusivist and pluralist positions alike, I cannot help feeling that the delicate balance I witnessed so clearly in the Guide—a balance of acceptance and rejection, welcome and critique, and now, we might add, insider and outsider—has been rather too sharply tipped in the direction of uncritical welcome and acceptance. Given the problematic history of Christian exclusivism, it is perfectly natural that we might tend to overcompensate in the other direction. But this tendency, natural though it may well be, should not prevent us

---

[21] On "practical pluralism," see Eck, *Encountering God*, 190–99.

[22] See the compelling arguments for retaining a lively appreciation for difference in J. A. DiNoia, O.P., *The Diversity of Religions: A Christian Perspective* (Washington, D.C.: The Catholic University of America Press, 1992); and S. Mark Heim, *Salvations: Truth and Difference in Religion* (Maryknoll, N.Y.: Orbis Books, 1995).

from seeking to recover the very balance and tension that may have been lost in the first place.

So the question becomes: where can we look for a better model? To attempt an answer, I turn once again to that masterpiece of Christian Scripture that has informed so many of the reflections in these pages: the Fourth Gospel. Toward the end of this Gospel narrative, after Jesus has been crucified and raised from the dead, we meet the same disciple Peter whom we encountered earlier in a passage from the Gospel of Mark. This time, however, it is not merely Peter who is singled out for special attention. For Peter is not alone:

> Peter turned and saw the disciple whom Jesus loved following them; he was the one who had reclined next to Jesus at the [last supper before Jesus' crucifixion] and had said, "Lord, who is it that is going to betray you?" When Peter saw him, he said to Jesus, "Lord, what about him?" Jesus said to him, "If it is my will that he remain until I come, what is that to you? Follow me!" (John 21:20-22).

In this cryptic scene, we witness a bit of rivalry between Peter, greatest of the disciples and symbolic leader of the early Church, and this straggler, referred to simply as "the disciple whom Jesus loved" or, more commonly, "the Beloved Disciple."

Now it is worth noting that the precise identity of this Beloved Disciple is a very murky issue for those who study the Fourth Gospel very attentively. Shortly after the passage quoted above, he is identified as the witness on whose testimony the Fourth Gospel is based (John 21:24-25), and Church tradition has identified this witness with John, one of the twelve disciples whom Jesus chose to represent the new community he was gathering around himself. Hence, the Fourth Gospel is also more typically referred to as the Gospel of John.

Not a few biblical scholars, however, question this identification of the Beloved Disciple as one of the Twelve. His rather abrupt appearance at the table of Jesus' Last Supper in John 13:23-26, along with the persistent reluctance of the Gospel writer to assign him a name, suggest that he is very likely *not* among those who have been previously named as Jesus' disciples.[23] At least one interpreter has, for example, suggested

---

[23] See discussion and references in Brown, *Community of the Beloved Disciple*, 31–34. For a comprehensive survey of the issue, see James H. Charlesworth, *The Beloved Disciple: Whose Witness Validates the Gospel of John?* (Valley Forge, Pa.: Trinity Press International, 1995).

that the Beloved Disciple may be Lazarus, who is himself raised from the dead shortly before the Last Supper, in chapter eleven of the Gospel narrative.[24] The great Catholic biblical commentator Raymond E. Brown makes another suggestion: perhaps this is the unnamed companion of Andrew in John 1:35-40, whom we have already encountered in the introduction to this book.[25]

In a sense, it doesn't really matter who exactly the Beloved Disciple was: his name, his background, and so on. What's more important is the basic fact that he seems to have been, in Brown's words, "an outsider to the group of best-known disciples."[26] When we further consider that the Beloved Disciple is, like Peter, serving a symbolic role in the narrative, representing the vision and heritage of the community that produced the Fourth Gospel—so different in tone and detail from the other three canonical Gospels—then we gain a better sense of what is at stake in this short passage. We have an outsider Gospel from an outsider community founded upon the teaching of someone who was himself an outsider.[27] And so, catching a glimpse of this outsider following along at the outskirts of the core group, Peter can only say, rather bluntly, "Lord, what about him?"

How does Jesus respond? Well, we can note a couple of things he does *not* do. He does not, first, say to Peter, "This straggler, this outsider, is really one of your own number, not to be excluded." That is, he does not attempt to include the Beloved Disciple amongst the more well-recognized disciples.[28] At the same time, Jesus does not withdraw anything from the unique promise and status given to these Twelve. Indeed, when he says "Follow me!" Jesus is not just issuing a bald command. He is reaffirming a series of similar injunctions that reinforce the authority and responsibility of Peter and the other apostles, especially in their shared ministry as teachers, pastors and witnesses to the truth: "Feed my lambs" (v. 15), "Tend my sheep" (v. 16), "Feed my sheep" (v. 17), and finally "Follow me" (v. 19). The insider remains an insider; the outsider remains an outsider.

---

[24] E.g., Vernard Eller, *The Beloved Disciple: His Name, His Story, His Thought: Two Studies from the Gospel of John* (Grand Rapids, Mich.: William B. Eerdmans Publishing Company, 1987).

[25] Brown, *Community of the Beloved Disciple*, 32–33. Also see above, pp. 5–7.

[26] Ibid., 34.

[27] See ibid., esp. 81–91.

[28] Although this is, in effect, what Church tradition *has* done, by identifying the Beloved Disciple with John, son of Zebedee.

So, if Jesus does not make the Beloved Disciple into an insider, what does he do? He replies to Peter's blunt "So what about him?" with an equally blunt retort: "If it is my will that he remain until I come, what is that to you?" The Beloved Disciple also has a vital role to play, a role that may even continue until the end of time, but that role does not require him to become an insider to the more well-known and established group of disciples. If Peter may be interpreted to object that this doesn't make sense or appears on the face of it to violate other things Jesus has previously done and promised, the response is simple: "What is that to you?" At the end of the day, God's saving designs may well be—in fact, certainly *are*—broader and deeper than even Peter can so easily imagine.

The outsider, then, remains an outsider. But it just may turn out that this very outsider is, in truth, a most holy and beloved disciple of God.

Placing Ourselves in Peter's Shoes

Before we proceed further, we should note that the Fourth Gospel is notoriously difficult to "enlist" for one or another theological position on the Church's relationship with other religions. For example, many of this Gospel's statements about Christ and Christian community are overtly exclusivist, providing ample fodder for the evangelical tracts that used to appear altogether too often on my car windshield. Consider the following words, uttered to Nicodemus toward the beginning of Jesus' ministry:

> Indeed, God did not send the Son into the world to condemn the world, but in order that the world might be saved through him. Those who believe in him are not condemned; but those who do not believe are condemned already, because they have not believed in the name of the only Son of God (John 3:17-18).

Elsewhere in the Gospel, Jesus will file down the sharp edges of this portrait just a bit, in terms that might be more congenial to an inclusivist interpretation:

> I am the good shepherd. I know my own and my own know me, just as the Father knows me and I know the Father. And I lay down my life for the sheep. I have other sheep that do not be-

long to this fold. I must bring them also, and they will listen to my voice. So there will be one flock, one shepherd (John 10:14-16).

Finally, while reclining at table just before his death, Jesus slips into a slightly more pluralist idiom. "Do not let your hearts be troubled," he reassures his disciples. "Believe in God, believe also in me. In my Father's house there are many dwelling places. If it were not so, would I have told you that I go to prepare a place for you?" (John 14:1-3).

In the face of these different kinds of statements with different kinds of consequences for Christian self-understanding, the reader of the Fourth Gospel might be tempted to *choose one* and somehow to bend the others to fit it. Or, at the other end of the spectrum, she might eventually throw up her hands in despair, thoroughly convinced that Christian teachings on these matters are fundamentally inconsistent and possibly even self-contradictory.

Somewhere in this tangled mess, far from either extreme, we may need to step into Peter's shoes, to pose the question in its bluntest form: "Lord, what about him?" Or, perhaps better: Lord, what about *them*, these others in our midst, the followers of religious paths and participants in religious institutions other than our own, whose commitment we see, recognize, and perhaps admire even as it distinguishes them profoundly from ourselves. How, exactly, are we to think about *them*?

If we do place ourselves in Peter's shoes and do ask the question in its bluntest form, we will no doubt hear, not exactly an explanation, but a gentle retort. Jesus may well pull these outsiders—these beloved disciples we do not and cannot ever completely recognize as fellow insiders to our shared communion—close to himself and reply, "What is that to you?" If it is God's will that these others remain and fulfill a vital role in God's saving purpose until the very end of time, what is that to us? Moreover, if we are properly attentive and if we steadfastly refuse to insulate ourselves or retreat behind the familiar boundaries of our cultures and our institutions, we may also discover that *we* are the outsiders. In some situations, it will be *our* belief and trust that separate us from a shared communion upon which we discover we have stumbled. Then it will be the Lord speaking these words on *our* behalf, rather than the other way around.

At such moments, we may well stop, look around ourselves, and realize that what we have stumbled across is not just a puzzling dilemma or frustrating paradox, but a spiritual tension with the power to nourish us even as it once again draws us beyond our otherwise legitimate understandings and expectations. We may indeed be in the midst of questions and confusions not entirely unlike those that motivated our spiritual pursuit in the first place. That is, we may find ourselves in the presence of profound *mystery*, a mystery that founds and underlies, not merely our individual spiritual journeys, but perhaps even the fundamental teachings of the great religious traditions themselves.[29]

When I try to find words to describe this mystery, a mystery that joins us to others even as it distinguishes us from them, I do not find myself turning to the language of pluralism or inclusivism. At the end of the day, these positions seem to give away too much of the distinctive risk and blossoming knowledge that ground and shape our commitments to our religious institutions. By placing our trust in a teacher or teachers and joining ourselves to fellow seekers in a shared effort of spiritual pursuit, we have also made ourselves outsiders to other teachers and other shared communions . . . and, in some definitive sense, made them outsiders to us. This cannot, at least to my way of thinking, be compromised. And so pluralism and inclusivism fall by the wayside.

At the same time, Christian traditions of exclusivism hold absolutely no appeal. Such traditions have again and again proven themselves disastrous, both to the Church and especially to those others whom it used every means at its disposal to convert or to exclude. I believe that *Nostra Aetate* and the "Baar Declaration," along with many other public documents from many other religious bodies, represent a very positive watershed moment in the life of the Church. There is no going back, and rightly so.

Where, then, does this leave us? In my personal judgment, it leaves us in the shoes of Peter, hearing Jesus' gentle retort and responding with the very same belief and trust that grounded our commitment to the religious institution in the first place, even if we *also* have to scratch our heads in bemusement. It leaves us with a Christian seeker and a Hindu teacher, facing one another as outsiders and nevertheless choosing to continue their shared study together. It leaves us with the bishops of the Second Vatican Council, insisting that Christians proclaim Christ as "the way, the truth, and the life" while at the same time preserving and

---

[29] Cf. Michael Horace Barnes, *In the Presence of Mystery: An Introduction to the Story of Human Religiousness*, rev. ed. (Mystic, Conn.: Twenty-Third Publications, 1990).

encouraging values and traditions that may well contradict this proclamation. It leaves us, finally, with the example of the Guide, who could faithfully witness and joyfully welcome my entrance into a life and community that, just perhaps, she herself judged to be ultimately incompatible with what is most promising, most true, and most faithful to the spiritual quest.

It leaves us, in short, with mystery.

A Mystery of Relationship

At this point, we receive some support and clarification from what might initially seem an unlikely quarter: the Congregation for the Doctrine of the Faith (CDF), known in darker moments of Catholic history as the Holy Office and even as the Inquisition. On September 5, 2000, this Vatican congregation issued a declaration entitled *Dominus Iesus*, "Lord Jesus," in large part to refute a "mentality of indifferentism" that does not grant to the Catholic Church a unique and nontransferable "fullness of the means of salvation."[30] As might be expected, the document was greeted with considerable dismay from the more progressive corners of Church and society.[31] Some news media outlets reported that the declaration had, in effect, confirmed the intuitions of my "Christian Faith" class by reasserting the old adage: *Extra ecclesiam nulla salus,* "No salvation outside the Church."

Once the dust settled, most interpreters came to see that the declaration's position was far more nuanced than such facile reporting allowed. Despite some very artificial distinctions and a defensive, almost hostile tone that quite naturally led many readers to suppose otherwise, *Dominus Iesus* did not roll back the teachings of the Second Vatican Council or exclude non-Catholics from either salvation or truth; in fact, the CDF cites with approval the council's teaching that God does indeed bestow "salvific grace" upon "individual non-Christians . . . 'in

---

[30] Congregation for the Doctrine of the Faith (CDF), *Dominus Iesus* 22, in CDF, "'Dominus Iesus': On the Unicity and Salvific Universality of Jesus Christ and the Church," *Origins* 30 (September 14, 2000) 218.

[31] For a range of different responses to the declaration, mainly from the U.S. context, see Stephen J. Pope and Charles Hefling, eds., *Sic et Non: Encountering Dominus Iesus* (Maryknoll, N.Y.: Orbis Books, 2002).

ways known to himself.'"[32] At the same time, the congregation is equally insistent that such grace comes to those outside the Church in a way that, in a phrase it borrows from Pope John Paul II, always "has a mysterious relationship to the church."[33]

Now, if the CDF quotes this papal formulation simply to indicate that there is much we don't understand about the relationship of Christians and the Church to religious others, then it has said little that does not describe *any* relationship. There is much that we don't understand about what joins us to our husbands, wives, or partners, to our friends or colleagues, and perhaps above all to those teachers on whose paths we have stumbled or will stumble in the course of our spiritual journeys. Relationships themselves are permeated with much that is mysterious and evades rational explanation.

Although my own experience amply supports the notion that interreligious relationships will always be "mysterious" in this ordinary sense, the members of the Vatican congregation seem to have more in mind when they employ the term in *Dominus Iesus*. Indeed, the document might be read to suggest that the truth and grace of other religious persons, and presumably also of their traditions (though the CDF generally restricts its attention to the former), cannot be understood by Christians *except* in relation to the Church. True and holy these persons, their traditions, and their institutions may be and certainly *are* in individual cases. This truth and holiness will always, however, manifest an indissoluble relation that joins such persons, traditions, and institutions to the Church even as it distinguishes them from it. And, precisely because this relation consists of a subtle balance of acceptance and rejection, joy and critique, mutual recognition and profound difference—because, in sum, it is a relation that brings religious persons and

---

[32] *Dominus Iesus* 21, in CDF, "'Dominus Iesus,'" 218. See James Fredericks, "The Catholic Church and the Other Religious Paths: Rejecting Nothing That Is True and Holy," *Theological Studies* 64 (2003) esp. 226–33. See also the International Theological Commission (ITC), "Christianity and the World Religions," *Origins* 27 (August 14, 1997) 159 (no. 63): "The primary question today is not whether men [sic] can attain salvation even if they do not belong to the visible Catholic Church; this possibility is considered theologically certain." It is worth noting that the CDF explicitly commends this ITC document in the synthesis that accompanied the release of *Dominus Iesus*. See Congregation for the Doctrine of the Faith, "Synthesis of the Declaration 'Dominus Iesus,'" *Origins* 30 (September 14, 2000) 221.

[33] *Dominus Iesus* 20–21, in CDF, "'Dominus Iesus,'" 217–18. Of course, this also depends upon the language of the Vatican II document *Lumen Gentium* 16, which describes non-Christians as "related in various ways" to the people of God. See Flannery, 21.

institutions together not as insiders, but as the outsiders they are and perhaps must continue to be in accord with God's saving designs[34]— because of all this, it can only be understood on the order of mystery.

That is not the end of the matter, however, at least not for me. For, once we have reached even a tentative conclusion that whatever draws us into relation with religious others is ultimately mysterious, we suddenly come across an intriguing point of contact with the Hindu teacher and the Christian bishop who have guided so many of our reflections thus far. In particular, we can observe that some mystery of relationship, broadly defined, stands close to the center of their respective visions of religious truth.

In the case of the former's tradition of Advaita Vedanta, one of the most pressing and elusive questions turns upon the precise relation between the world and God. In her own study of Shankara and Thomas Aquinas, for example, philosopher and inculturationist Sara Grant has characterized this relation as a "non-reciprocal dependence relation," a relation that places God at the root and foundation of the world while preserving God's transcendence and ultimate independence from this same world.[35] How is this possible? It is possible, we can gather from Shankara, only if their mutual relation is, at some level, assigned to mystery.

It is important to note at the outset that, for Shankara, "world" and "God" are not primarily understood in the abstract, as philosophical categories. They represent, instead, issues of urgent personal concern. If I am ultimately nondifferent from *brahman,* God the divine Self, how do I account for all those experiences in life that suggest I am a finite individual, with a body, mind, and personality? How do I account for pain and death? If I am actually God, free from all suffering and limitation, how can I understand "the world" as I experience it?

In the prose portion of *A Thousand Teachings,* Shankara characterizes this paradoxical union of opposite claims—this apparent coincidence of limitless *brahman* and limited personality, of eternal God and

---

[34] For Christian attempts to understand how other religious traditions can be read as playing a positive role in God's plan, see Dupuis, *Toward a Christian Theology of Religious Pluralism,* esp. 330–57; and S. Mark Heim, *The Depth of the Riches* (Grand Rapids, Mich., and Cambridge, Mass.: William B. Eerdmans Publishing Company, 2001).

[35] Sara Grant, R.S.C.J., *Toward an Alternative Theology: Confessions of a Non-Dualist Christian* (Notre Dame, Ind.: University of Notre Dame Press, 2002) 40–43.

an all too temporal world—in two mutually supporting ways.[36] First, he offers his own version of Jesus' statement, "What is that to you?" when he traces the ultimate origin of the world of ordinary experience to God's *achintya-shakti,* "inconceivable power," something not unlike a transcendent, unfathomable, divine prerogative. In other words, the inscrutable juxtaposition of God and world, divine Self and limited personality, finds its most fundamental cause in Mystery properly so-called: the overarching, undergirding, and all-pervasive mystery of God as God, as the transcendent source and end of all being.

Shankara could stop there, I suppose, but he does not. Instead, he specifies this mystery further as a relation between God and an "everything else" defined as *tattva-anyatvabhyam anirvacaniya,* "indescribable either as That [God] or as other [than That]." He introduces the analogy of foam on the surface of the water to illustrate the relation: just as foam has no existence apart from water and yet is not quite the same as water itself, so also our experiences in the world have an indeterminate status. They are ultimately inseparable and thus nondifferent from God the divine Self, who is also our own true self. At the same time, such experiences have their own integrity and distinctive characteristics— they are temporal, susceptible to change and suffering, and so on—that render them unlike and, in a sense, contradictory to God. They are *tattva-anyatvabhyam anirvacaniya,* indefinable as absolutely the same or absolutely different, existing in and through a mysterious relationship to the one limitless and eternal God.

Later Advaita tradition would take this description by Shankara and render it into an abstract noun: *anirvacaniyatva* or "indeterminableness."[37] And, for many if not most Advaitins, this notion of *anirvacaniyatva* represents a lynchpin in the whole nondualist religious vision. With the acceptance that worldly experience is indeterminable as either the same as or separate from God, many other aspects of the teaching fall right into place. Without it (or something like it), on the other hand, the apparent contradictions between the truth of *advaita* and the evident facts of ordinary experience remain just that: contradic-

---

[36] I am confining my treatment here to Shankara, *A Thousand Teachings,* Prose Portion 1.18-19, in Jagadananda, 11–12 (slightly modified).

[37] See Daniel H. H. Ingalls, "Samkara on the Question: 'Whose is avidya?'" *Philosophy East and West* 3/1 (1953) esp. 69–70.

tions.[38] In the absence of this mysterious relationship between God and world, the tradition itself risks incoherence and absurdity.

If we shift our attention to the Christian side of the conversation, we do not have to look very far for a central mystery without which the religious tradition risks absurdity and incoherence. In his treatise *On Instructing the Uninstructed,* for example, Augustine draws an analogy to the incarnation of Jesus the Christ to offer encouragement to the catechist who has grown weary of her own words:

> . . . let us consider what has been vouchsafed to us beforehand by Him *who showed us an example, that we should follow His steps* [1 Pet 2:21]. For however widely our spoken word differs from the rapidity of our understanding, greater by far is the difference between mortal flesh and equality with God. And yet, *though He was in the* same *form, He emptied himself, taking the form of a servant,* etc., *even to the death of the cross.*[39]

The final passage to which Augustine alludes is one of the great christological hymns in the letters of the apostle Paul, in which Jesus the Christ is described as the one

> who, though he was in the form of God,
> did not regard equality with God as something to be exploited,
> but emptied himself, taking the form of a slave,
> being born in human likeness.
> And being found in human form,
> he humbled himself and became obedient to the point of death—
> even death on a cross (Phil 2:6-8).

This is that highest mystery without which Christianity falls flat and fallow: Christ, proclaimed by Christians as God the divine Self, who comes down from the heights of divinity and becomes a human being for the salvation of all humankind.

What's most striking about Augustine's phrase, however, is the way he characterizes the mystery of the Incarnation as a joining of apparent contraries, or the closing of an otherwise unbridgeable gap between

---

[38] Cf. Martha J. Doherty, "A Contemporary Debate in Advaita Vedanta: Avidya and the Views of Swami Satchidanandendra Saraswati" (Ph.D. diss., Harvard University, 1999).

[39] Augustine of Hippo, *On Instructing the Uninstructed* 10.15, in Christopher, 37.

"mortal flesh" on the one hand and "equality with God" on the other—
that is, as a kind of relationship. Later tradition would define this mystery in explicitly relational terms, speaking of the one person Jesus the
Christ through a juxtaposition or union of two "natures," human and
divine. Not entirely unlike Shankara's use of the negation *tattva-
anyatva-bhyam anirvacaniya* to describe the relation of the world to
God, the ecumenical Council of Chalcedon would in 451 C.E. offer a
series of qualifiers that define this union of natures in Christ by defining what it is not: human and divine are brought together "without
confusion, without change, without division, without separation."[40]

Here we encounter yet another mysterious relationship at the center
of the tradition, a relationship that preserves the integrity and otherness
of each side even as it rejects separation or division.[41] Apparent irrecon-
cilables are brought together into an intimate, saving relation without
collapsing one into the other or giving up the distinctive qualities or
claims of either side. It may appear contradictory, but Christians vehe-
mently insist that this is not the case. It is, instead, a saving truth that
can be endlessly investigated without ever being exhausted.[42] It is, in
many respects, *the* great mystery of the faith. And it is entirely wrapped
up in this vital notion of *relationship*.

A Different Kind of Harmony?

Of course, for at least some members of our societies, calling something a "mystery" is not really very different from throwing up our
hands. It could be regarded as a tacit admission that Advaitin teaching
doesn't make much sense in the face of everyday experience, for example, or that Christians want to have their cake and eat it too when it
comes to explaining Jesus the Christ. We can't figure something out,
something vitally important to ourselves and our religious traditions.
What do we do? We declare the issue in question out of bounds for
rational inquiry, cordon it off, and label it "mystery." Such a strategy

---

[40] Bernhard Lohse, *A Short History of Christian Doctrine: From the First Century to the Present*, rev. ed., trans. Ernest Stoeffler (Philadelphia: Fortress Press, 1985) 92.

[41] Cf. David Lochhead, *The Dialogical Imperative: A Christian Reflection on Interfaith Encounter*, Faith Meets Faith Series (Maryknoll, N.Y.: Orbis Books, 1988) 92–97.

[42] See Michael J. Himes, *Doing the Truth in Love: Conversations about God, Relationships and Service* (New York/Mahwah: Paulist Press, 1995) esp. 83–87.

might be interpreted as a veiled admission that, at the end of the day, the various disparate assertions of our religious traditions inevitably draw us into a bit of a muddle.

There have been uncharitable moments in my own reading of the declaration *Dominus Iesus* when I judged that the Vatican congregation was doing just this—that assigning the relationship between the Church and non-Christians to "mystery" was a theologically sophisticated way of trying to kill the conversation in impatient and largely ignorant disgust. A reading that is more generous to the congregation and perhaps more faithful to Shankara and Augustine's disparate notions of a mysterious relation at the heart of each tradition, however, may lead us in another direction altogether. It may lead us to a point at which the mere label "mystery" cannot properly be interpreted to diminish the importance of relationships that stretch the boundaries of religious traditions. It may, in fact, do just the opposite.

Indeed, if the relationship that joins religious others to our own shared communion is truly a mystery in the highest sense of the term— a mystery no less central and definitive than the mysterious relation of God and creation in Advaita Vedanta, or the saving mystery of the incarnation of Christ in Christian tradition—then active engagement of this mystery through dialogue and collaboration may not be an incidental add-on to our institutional commitment. In the absence of such dialogue and cooperation, institutional commitment itself may well risk incoherence and absurdity.

But even here we have not reached the end of our inquiry or the depths of the mystery it reveals. For an odd and unexpected conclusion naturally follows: namely, that we come into the presence of this mystery only insofar as we have been willing to risk the complex dynamic of belief and trust that joins us to our religious traditions and institutions in the first place. That is, we enter this profound mystery *in and through* our conviction and commitment, *not* despite them. Conviction and commitment are what make true relationship—a relationship between outsiders who have plunged their roots deep into quite different soils— a living principle of our lives, rather than just a nice idea.

I count myself very lucky that this living principle was presented to me, not after many years as a practicing Catholic, but at the very moment I made my commitment to the religious institution. As already noted, many of those who influenced my decision to be baptized in the Church were not themselves Catholic. A beautiful irony of my baptism, confirmation, and First Communion was the fact that, from among this number of non-Catholics, the person who was by far the harshest *critic* of my decision was also one of very few who actually showed up to witness the event itself. Now, after many years of reflection, I think I see in the Guide's presence much more than a reluctant favor from a music professor for an enthusiastic student. The Guide understood and appreciated my commitment to the institution precisely because she understood and appreciated her own values and commitments. And so I see in her presence and joyful witness a bond of mutual recognition and respect, a bond that joined us together even as it drew us apart. I see, in other words, a mystery of relationship.

In the previous chapter of this study, I suggested that the bond that joins us to others in a shared communion represents a kind of harmony of spiritual pursuit. Now, in the context of our journey in this chapter, it might be said that our relationships with religious others can also represent a kind of harmony. But this will be a harmony of a different kind altogether. Instead of the almost mathematical order and precision we get in one of Johann Sebastian Bach's well-known fugues or one of Wolfgang Amadeus Mozart's popular symphonies, we will have the long silences, strange cadences, or highly compressed arrangements of a John Cage, a Laurie Anderson, or an Arnold Schoenberg. It will be a harmony of apparent disharmony, a musical adventure that transgresses the familiar and well-trodden path.

Confronted with a work like Cage's "Four Minutes, Thirty-Three Seconds," in which a lone pianist sits quietly for the duration of the piece, leaving us to appreciate the occasional creaks and coughs of the audience as "music," we might be tempted to dismiss what we hear and leave the performance hall dissatisfied and annoyed. Or we might be so enamored of the piece's novelty that we give up Bach and Mozart altogether. Neither option would, to my way of thinking, truly honor the manifold ways such experiments with new musical styles can both presume and nourish our deeper appreciation for what is already familiar and closer to home. With this analogy in mind, we might do well to nourish and appreciate our commitments to our own religious institutions more deeply, while at the same time pressing the boundaries of these institutions and stretching our visions of these very commitments. In the process, we will better understand who we are even as we enter into the lives and understandings of others.

This, it seems to me, was the greatest lesson offered by the Guide: a vision of harmony that once again, as at the beginning of our search, calls us relentlessly beyond our otherwise legitimate hopes and expectations. If we respond to this call, what will we discover? It is impossible to know in advance. But, if we are sincere and attentive in our pursuit, we may well discover that we are participants in a much greater achievement of harmony, a bold and surprising musical tour de force composed by that great Musician Herself, the unfathomable source and end of all spiritual life and human fulfillment.

And so, just perhaps, the Guide did teach me something about music after all.

Conclusion

Filling in the Gaps

The Big Gap

When the manuscript for this book was in its early stages, I showed it to several friends and teachers for comment. Although I credit quite a lot of whatever may be truly worthwhile in these pages to feedback from these readers, one of them made a particularly astute observation relatively late in the process. Considering that the work draws so deeply upon personal encounters with significant teachers, he noted, it was rather remarkable that one could read it without discovering that I had spent the better part of a decade in seminary and graduate school. In all of my years studying theology with a wide variety of professors and colleagues, were there no experiences sufficiently vivid to include in this volume?

I can't remember exactly how I responded to this comment when it was made, but I've thought about it quite a bit since then. There are some fairly pedestrian reasons I could offer to explain the apparent anomaly, of course. Professor and Priest, Guru and Guide—these were decisive figures in my spiritual journey, but they were also persons who, coincidentally, generated stories that nicely illustrated the issues I set out to discuss in this book. All of them, moreover, journeyed with me at what happened to be points of great transition and discovery. My initial commitment to the Church came together at precisely the time I stumbled across the paths of the Professor, Priest, and Guide, and at no other time has this commitment been challenged and refined as it was during my brief period of study with the Guru, some ten years later. This just happens to be the way my life and my institutional commitment have worked themselves out.

Nevertheless, I find myself thinking of the period that elapsed between these two stages in my journey, a period rich in its own unanticipated insights and bumbling errors, as well as the sure guidance of extraordinary mentors and fellow travelers on the way, as "the Big Gap." This work is as much the fruit of *these* insights, errors, and guidance as any experiences with the Guru, Guide, Priest, and Professor. But they are not, nor shall be, part of the narrative in these pages. They sit fruitfully in between, securely ensconced in the Big Gap. They deeply influence my thinking and feeling about everything I have written here, despite the fact that they escape explicit mention.

From that Big Gap pointed out by my reader, moreover, I also find my attention drawn to those many other "little gaps" of our spiritual journeys, all those unmentioned and perhaps even unrecognized experiences, factors, and influences that shape who we are and what we might even think *to mention* in the first place. Our lives are broad canvases with many wrinkles and folds; it would be impossible to capture *everything* in our own minds, much less on a written page. Most of it inevitably remains in the gaps.

Filling in a Few Gaps

Not so long ago, I was confronted in a small, dramatic way with some of those gaps that have deeply influenced both my experiences themselves and also the ways I have tried to synthesize and present them in this book.

The event in question took place in the middle of August, on a small college campus in New Jersey. On behalf of my own college, which was founded by the Sisters of Mercy, I was attending a gathering of representatives from Mercy-sponsored institutions of higher education throughout the United States. On this particular morning, conference participants filed dutifully into a large lecture hall to hear about the theological foundations of service learning in the Mercy tradition.

There was much in the presentation that morning worthy of note: the speaker, herself a Sister of Mercy and theologian of some repute, offered an exceptionally compelling exposition of the Catholic and Mercy spirit that could and should infuse our various institutions. More importantly for our purposes here, she did so with specific reference to the meeting of Jesus and the Samaritan woman described in the Fourth Gospel, a scene which I treated in some detail in chapter 2.[1] Having only recently completed that piece of writing, I listened to her interpretation with great interest and enthusiasm. Like me, I noticed gladly, the presenter unfolded the story primarily as a meeting of teacher and student. *Unlike* me, however, she took great care to point out how clever and insightful a dialogue partner the Samaritan woman is for Jesus, in places leading him to what might be a higher understanding of his own ministry and significance. By the end of the presentation, I began to suspect that I had rather dramatically underplayed the Samaritan woman's role in this biblical text and had thus smothered a significant theme of mutuality between teacher and student—a theme that permeates the entire episode.

I discovered, in other words, that my interpretation and understanding of the Fourth Gospel reveals its own significant gaps.

My instinct in a situation like this is to plead ignorance, to hide behind the fact that I am not primarily trained as a biblical scholar, or to point out that I never claimed that my interpretations were comprehensive or complete. These disclaimers are true enough, but they only scratch the surface. For the gaps in my interpretation follow from those other gaps we've already touched on, the gaps in our lives and journeys themselves.

What are some of these gaps? Well, the most important gaps in my life probably remain unnoticed or unacknowledged, but a few do emerge into fairly clear view.

I think, for example, of the years immediately after my undergraduate studies, when I served as a volunteer teacher and aide at a Jesuit school in Pine Ridge, South Dakota. At this reservation school, I confronted many of my own weaknesses as a person and educator at the same moment I witnessed more than a few profound intersections of the Catholic Church with the native Lakota religion and culture. It was a time of tremendous desolation, consolation, and grace on my spiritual journey. Indeed, my experiences on the reservation could probably fill a book in and of themselves.

---

[1] See above, pp. 46–50.

But they never will. For, on one unremarkable afternoon in the high school teachers' lounge, I had a conversation about my hopes, my dreams, and especially my writing with the head custodian of the schools. This Lakota man, whom I learned to respect more than most people I have met before or since that time, leaned back in his chair. "Just do me one favor," he said. "Don't write about your experiences on the reservation. Honestly, there are just too many white people doing that already."

I agreed without hesitation, and I hope and pray that I remain—despite brief exceptions like these few paragraphs—faithful to my word.

A second example also springs to mind: the vibrant community of Aikiya Alayam, "Temple of Unity," in Chennai. This Jesuit seminary and dialogue center served as my home throughout my studies with the Guru, and the Indian priests and seminarians with whom I lived received me so generously that the vaunted "Southern hospitality" of my home began to seem rather pale and silly in comparison—unless, that is, "Southern" might be revised to mean "South Indian"! At the same time, I could not help but sense mild disapproval for the project I was undertaking. There was no problem with the fact that I was engaging in interreligious dialogue; the Jesuits of South Asia are well-recognized leaders in this ever more prominent feature of the Church's ongoing mission and theological reflection. Nor did my hosts ever question my choice to study with the Guru himself, whom they readily accepted as a holy person and able guide.

No, things were considerably more subtle at Aikiya Alayam, and so it took me a while to piece them together. After a couple of visits to the outlying villages where the seminarians ministered every weekend, however, I slowly realized what should have been obvious all along: namely, that these Jesuits specifically and deliberately took upon themselves the perspectives of the oppressed *dalit* or outcaste segments of Indian society. Add to this ministry a certain Tamil resistance to the Sanskrit-based culture associated with the north of the country, and what emerged was an underlying, rarely spoken critique of the Advaita tradition as a *symbol* of Sanskrit culture generally and of the Brahmin caste in particular. The good-natured laughs when our spicy meals made me hiccup, the anxious discussions about the rise of Hindu nationalism in Indian political life, and several earnest pleas not to neglect the rich folk cultures and indigenous traditions of Tamil Nadu in my pursuit of interreligious dialogue—behind all of these otherwise unrelated encounters lay an assumption I think all of us recognized though it went unvoiced. I was an American, a person of privilege. I had come to India to pursue the study of Advaita Vedanta, a tradition which my hosts could not help but connect with its own history of privilege and oppression. It was, perhaps sadly, an all too perfect fit.

The final "gap" that I will discuss in these pages is both more personal and more recent. About a decade after my service in Pine Ridge and two years after my trip to India, I was living in central Minnesota and writing my dissertation. Whenever I could, I drove into the Twin Cities to visit an old friend, whom I had actually first met as a fellow volunteer on the reservation those many years before. I regarded her, then as now, as my moral compass, close friend, and trusted confidante. So, when I found myself in Minneapolis on one particularly cold weekend in early February, we quite naturally took the visit as an opportunity to celebrate her birthday by taking in a movie.

I still don't know exactly what happened that Saturday evening, after the film. One moment, we were just sitting comfortably in her living room, sipping beer and waiting for a couple of other companions to arrive. Before I knew it and for no apparent reason, I suddenly found myself confessing some of my deepest secrets and darkest fears. In particular, I revealed a frightening suspicion that my most intimate relationships to that point, although certainly free of physical violence, were still somehow tainted with a hurtful pattern of lashing out and condemnation, a pattern that might haunt me for the rest of my days despite my best intentions to the contrary. I believe I may have posed an unfair question: "Is it possible that I am somehow destined to hurt the women I love?"

The question hung in the air for weeks. My friend really never had a chance to reply properly; as it happened, our companions arrived at precisely the moment I finished my confession. The next day, she expressed appropriate concern, assuring me that at least some of my fears seemed genuinely unfounded while also warning me sternly against any kind of complacency about the buried emotions they might represent. Quite a while later, I was able to trace a series of events—a few of which, on reflection, had genuinely little to do with me or my intentions—that had led to this outburst of self-pity and frustration in the first place. This realization gave me a small amount of comfort and reassurance. Yet another mutual friend of ours even suggested to me, weeks later, that it was my penchant for melodramatic pronouncements I should be watching, rather than anything specific to intimacy. But I couldn't shake the feeling that at least some small part of my fears had hit a little too close to home.

For, on that frigid weekend in February, it seemed to me that I had, by that confession itself, hurtfully clouded my good friend's enjoyment of her own birthday.

Gaps and Limits

These are just three of the "little gaps" in my life and spiritual journey, a very small sampling of what could be a virtually unending list of those more complex, ambiguous experiences that permeate and underlie the main narratives I have offered in these pages. In part, they are confessions of weakness, of moments when I was forced to see how short my life fell of the clarity and consistency I might wish for it. In fact, I *do* struggle—and not always successfully—to make my longed-for ideals the governing principles of my own life. It's more comfortable to render equity, justice, and love in beautiful prose than in concrete action, after all. As common wisdom would have it, it is far easier to "talk the talk" than to "walk the walk."

This assessment is true, as far as it goes. But I think such little gaps reveal more than just personal weakness. They reveal what feminists and other liberationist interpreters have come to call "social location." That is, they reveal the author of this book as an Anglo-American Catholic male, as a person who can speak very easily about dialogue and sharing in part because his most treasured religious and cultural traditions are not currently at risk of extinction or wholesale exploitation; who can use his leisure to craft analogies for spiritual hunger in part because he has never been reduced to starvation by the oppressive economic structures of his society; and who can speak of sexism not only as a theoretical idea at work "out there" somewhere, but as a reality of his own life and relationships. *Of course,* my interpretation of the Fourth Gospel differs from the one offered by that exceptional presenter who was also a woman and a member of a religious order committed to the poor and oppressed of this world. There may well be aspects of the text that, without her help, I literally could not see, due in no small part to who I am and where I happen to be "located" by gender, class, and ethnicity. I am selectively blinded by my little gaps, as are we all.

How to address this situation? There are moments when I believe the best response is the silence urged upon me by the head custodian of that Jesuit school in Pine Ridge. If voices like mine have too long dominated a public conversation, it might be best to fall silent and let others have their say.

Well, the discerning reader can tell by the simple fact of the book in your hands that I did not choose this option, at least not this time. But this leaves the challenge unanswered. If not silence, then what? An alternative response might be accommodation, an attempt to incorporate a broader range of perspectives and voices in my own work. Are there aspects of the Fourth Gospel I have missed? Then show me. Teach me to see more clearly, so that I can represent your concerns as well as mine.

As a theologian whose thinking leans a bit to the eclectic and synthetic side, I have the most sympathy for accommodation, and I am bold to believe that I *have* attempted to include at least some alternative voices as I conducted my research and put my ideas into writing. But I did not go back and revise my interpretation of the Fourth Gospel in the wake of that conference in mid-August, and I have not really attempted to reassess and revise my understanding of spirituality *itself*, at least not in any sustained way. And so questions remain. Are my primary sources too otherworldly and abstract? Are they too detached from immediate concerns of justice and equity, here and now? Have I succumbed to an unconscious bias in favor of individualistic and private conceptions of spiritual fulfillment?

These are important questions, but any credible attempt to answer them would certainly transform, and probably also enlarge, a slim volume such as this one. So I decided instead to say what I had to say, and to unfold the narrative from within a perspective that is, for better or for worse, steadfastly my own, severely limited by my social location and by what I am sure must be a host of selective biases and missed opportunities. Instead of silence or accommodation, then, I offer what I hope is authentic candor and appropriate modesty. My perspective is certainly limited, no question about that. And so I offer it *precisely as limited,* as one voice among all those which could or should be heard on the tangled, complicated, and often messy questions of spirituality and institutional commitment.[2]

---

[2] To name just a few titles that have been personally influential on my own journey: Leonardo Boff, *Saint Francis: A Model for Human Liberation,* trans. John W. Diercksmeier (New York: Crossroad Publishing Company, 1982); Denise Lardner Carmody, *An Ideal Church: A Meditation* (New York/Mahwah: Paulist Press, 1999); Elizabeth A. Johnson,

And so, where finally does this leave us? I think it leaves us with the words of the Upanishads, first quoted in the introduction:

> Take, for example, son, a person who is brought here blind-folded from the land of Gandhara and then left in a deserted region. As he was brought blindfolded and left there blind-folded, he would drift about there towards the east, or the north, or the south. Now, if someone were to free him from his blindfold and tell him, "Go that way; the land of Gandhara is in that direction," being a learned and wise person, he would go from village to village asking for directions and finally arrive in the land of Gandhara. In exactly the same way in this world when one has a teacher, he knows: "There is delay for me here only until I am freed; but then I will arrive!"[3]

Our considerations leave us, in other words, with the various journeys we ourselves have undertaken or will undertake, along with the many teachers and fellow companions who have guided or will guide our steps along the way. These journeys may well be limited, but they are *the journeys we have undertaken* nonetheless. And so we trust that, despite or even *through* their apparent limitations, they may yet lead us onward to the freedom for which we so desperately yearn.

Spiritual and *Religious?*

It seems obvious that the most prominent spiritual journey in this book is also by far the most limited: it is the journey we have attempted to trace in these pages themselves. This journey began, in the introduction, with that thoroughly ordinary yet profoundly mysterious moment of recognition that joined two then-anonymous seekers to Jesus of Nazareth, to a teacher inexplicably well suited to satisfy their innermost questions and desires. Eventually, after a long and circuitous route that brought us into contact with many different students, teachers, and

---

Friends of God and Prophets: A Feminist Theological Reading of the Communion of Saints (New York: Continuum Publishing Company, 1998); Carolyn Osiek, R.C.S.J., *Beyond Anger: On Being a Feminist in the Church* (New York/Mahwah: Paulist Press, 1986); and Aloysius Pieris, S.J., *An Asian Theology of Liberation,* Faith Meets Faith Series (Maryknoll, N.Y.: Orbis Books, 1988).

[3] Chandogya Upanishad 6.14.1-2, in Olivelle, *Upanisads,* 155 (slightly modified).

tangled questions of institutional commitment, we arrived at a deeper and more properly theological sense of mystery. It is a mystery that simultaneously distinguishes and draws together apparent contraries, in the very persons of all those who participate in diverse religious traditions and institutions. And, I tried to suggest, such a mystery of relationship may well represent an essential, even defining feature of the very convictions and commitments that join us to religious institutions in the first place.

Of course, strictly speaking, our shared journey didn't actually begin with a passage from the Fourth Gospel or from the Upanishads, or even with the journey itself. It began with a question about spirituality and religious institutions, with a challenge posed to institutional commitment above all by the rather modest place of Christianity among the great religious traditions of the world. Is it possible, or even preferable, to be spiritual but not religious? This volume's short interpretative journey has been offered as my tentative response to the question: an attempt to show how spirituality, in its fullest sense, finds expression in and through an appropriately balanced institutional commitment, rather than some other way. But I have also tried to show how such an appropriately balanced commitment, in *its* fullest sense, also opens into interreligious dialogue and collaboration. If, in my view, to be spiritual *is necessarily* to be religious, then it is also true that to be religious *is necessarily* to be in dialogue.

Now, there will always be more than one reason to engage in interreligious dialogue and cooperation, along with many ways to understand such dialogue and cooperation once they have begun. At moments, our most valuable models will be the prophetic voices of such organizations as the Federation of Asian Bishops' Conferences or such individuals as Paul Knitter and Diana Eck, prophetic voices that fearlessly identify the beloved outsiders in our midst as valued collaborators in a shared task of social and spiritual liberation from all that keeps our sisters and brothers enslaved. The needs of the world are very great, and we will certainly make little progress without the help and correction of others whom we simply *must* recognize as equals to ourselves. Despite this, there may also be moments when we instead follow the model of such broad-minded thinkers as Karl Rahner or those like him both inside and outside the Christian tradition. That is, we may find ourselves unable to see religious others as anything but *insiders* to that which, within our own traditions and institutions, we identify as the highest source and end of spiritual pursuit. There may even be moments when we look to such authoritative voices as Shankara, Augustine, and perhaps also the framers of *Dominus Iesus* to remind us that these religious others are nevertheless, and must in some sense remain, outsiders to us and we outsiders to them.

All of these models are valuable, and each contributes something to our understanding of both institutional commitment and the interreligious relationships that such commitment—at least in our contemporary world—will necessarily entail. In the previous chapter, however, I also tried to develop a few other models for our understanding: Jesus the Christ, responding to Peter's puzzled questioning with a gentle rebuff; the Advaitin notion of *anirvacaniyatva* or "indeterminableness," which explains the existence of worldly experience by explaining what it is not; and the same Jesus the Christ once again, this time understood theologically as a single person in two natures, related to one another in a way that defies confusion or change, separation or division. And finally, at least in my mind, each of these models leads in obvious or subtle ways to that model par excellence, the example set for me by the Guide. In the face of examples such as these, we might indeed come to understand ourselves in an intrinsic, mysterious relationship not only with a tradition and religious institution we eventually come to call our own, but also with all those religious others in our midst, those beloved outsiders who walk a journey and share a communion that is neither entirely foreign nor entirely recognizable as our own. We may find ourselves in the presence of profound mystery.

If any readers have found this account of things at all attractive, however, a further question might also emerge in their minds: where do we start? How do we plunge into this mystery and make the mysterious relationships it promises our own? The answer to such questions is, I think, always the same. Where do we start? We start wherever we happen to find ourselves, with the questions and confusions we have up to this point been reluctant to admit perhaps even to ourselves. We look carefully for those teachers in our midst, those gurus or guides, priests or professors who might be able to point the way beyond what we might otherwise expect.

Where do we start? With ourselves, certainly, but also with others. We enter this mystery of relationship, quite simply, by seeking out living relationships, by seeking out that shared communion that will carry us to the farther shore of our most cherished hopes and desires. We start right here and right now, with those people who surround us—or who might eventually come to surround us—right here and right now.

And how, we might also finally realize, could we ever have expected that it would happen some other way?

Getting Started

Of course, if we really do start right here and right now, it also means that we are always just getting started. The most important tasks lie ahead, and the most important steps on our shared journey are those that have yet to be taken.

Where do we start? Well, I started with the Professor, and so it is in the presence of the Professor that I still in some sense remain, every single day. Faced with difficult questions about Hinduism and Christianity, questions that cut to the heart of institutional commitment and the Church, this remarkable sage offered a thin, enigmatic smile. With a twinkle in his eye, he pronounced an answer to those who claimed that nothing—or, at least, nothing of any enduring value—really distinguishes Christians from anyone else.

"Christ." That's all. Just one word.

This one word would eventually drive me, not only to the Priest and, through him, into the Roman Catholic Church, but also into the fine arts building and the office of the Guide, to India and the feet of the Guru, to a mission school on a South Dakota reservation, to seminary, graduate study, and a dissertation, to a teaching career in theology and religion. Step by step, my journey has brought me closer to the heart of the mystery, closer to understanding what the Professor might, consciously or unconsciously, have meant by that single, intriguing word.

And yet my journey has only, just now, really begun.

Index of Subjects and Names

Adhikara, see fitness

Advaita: as nondualism, 56–57, 118–19; as a *sampradaya* or teaching tradition, 39, 68, 75, 85, 90–91, 117–19, 128–29; and "qualified nondualism" *(vishishta-advaita)*, 84 (n.27), 100–1; *see also brahman,* self-knowledge

Aikiya Alayam (Temple of Unity), 128–29

Anirvacaniyatva, see indeterminableness

Ark, Noah's, 74–75

Augustine of Hippo, Saint: on conversion, 30–34; on spiritual seekers, 35; on the paradoxical status of the teacher, 41–42; on belief, 42–46; on the inadequate teacher, 52–53; on apostolic succession, 58; on love in the instructional process, 70–71; and Noah's ark as a symbol of the Church, 74–75; on spiritual rebirth in baptism, 81–82, 84; and Christian exclusivism, 98–99; on the Incarnation, 119–20

Authority, 39–44, 57–60

Baar Statement, 105–6

Balance of acceptance and rejection, 97, 102, 109–12, 114–17

Bala Vidya Mandir, 63–64, 67, 68

Belief: as necessary, 42–43; as a feature of ordinary life, 43–44; as natural and spontaneous, 45–46; and the person of the teacher, 48–51; and questioning, 52–53; as source of disagreement, 97–98, 100–1; *see also* commitment

Beloved Disciple, 110–12

Bharati Theertha Mahaswamigal, Jagadguru Shri (Shankaracharya of Shringeri), 65–66

Boat of knowledge, *see* raft of knowledge

Bondage, 54–56, *see also* freedom

Brahman: as nondifferent from the self, 17, 56–57, 117; the knower of, 51–52, 73; body of *(brahma-sharira),* 83–84; *see also* God

Brahmin class, 19–20, 128

Brown, Raymond E., 111

Cage, John, 122–23

Chalcedon, ecumenical Council of, 120

Chanting, Vedic, 63–67

Church, Christian: as religious institution, 3–4, 69, 75, 79–80, 84–85, 90–91, 121–22; as worshipping community, 4, 75–76; as universal, 4 (n.1), 88–89, 102–3, 105–6; and Roman Catholicism, 4 (n.1), 14–5, 86–88, 93–96, 101–5; as goal of conversion, 31–32, 98–99; and broken trust, 40; as defined by mutual love, 71; as recipient of divine promise, 76–77; as mother of Christians, 81–82; and sexism, 95–96; other religious traditions' relation to, 102–5, 115–17; *see also* community, institutions

Collaboration, interreligious, *see* dialogue

Commitment, 4–5, 53–54, 57–61, 73–74, 80, 90–91, 95–96, 114, 121–23; *see also* belief

Communion, ecclesiology of, 86–89; stretching the boundaries of, 105–10

Community, vii, 15–16, 68–69, 74–75, 77–79, 88–89, 105, *see also* Church

Confessions, The, 30–33, 52–53, *see also* Augustine of Hippo

Congregation for the Doctrine of the Faith (CDF), *see Dominus Iesus*

Congruenter, see fitness

Continuity *(santati),* 68–69, 82–83, 89

Conversion, 30–34

Conviction, *see* commitment

Crew, rowing, 71–73, 79–80

Cyprian of Carthage, 98

Death, 21, 27–30

Desire, 21–26, 28–29, 31–36, 44

Dialogue, interreligious, 104–9, 121–23, 133–35

Disgust, sense of *(nirveda),* 21–24

Dominus Iesus (Declaration on the Unicity and Salvific Universality of Jesus Christ and the Church), 115–17, 121

Eck, Diana, 106, 108–9, 133

Eucharist, 87–88

Exclusivism, 97–102, 112, 114

Extra ecclesiam nulla salus, 98, 115

Faith, *see* belief

Family, 80–86, 91

Federation of Asian Bishops' Conferences, 108, 133

Feminism, 94–96, 130

Fitness: of the seeker *(adhikara),* 18–20, 34; of the grace of conversion (given *congruenter),* 32–34

Fluency, 45–47, 50–51, 85–86

Freedom, 7–8, 17, 38–39, 54–57, 73–74, 81–84

Friendship, 45–46, 85–86

Gaps, 125–32

Garbage: as musical group, 22–23; as beautiful, 23–24, 30

God, 6, 15–16, 27, 33–34, 41–42, 48, 56–57, 77–78, 81–82, 100, 117–20, 123; *see also brahman*

Grant, Sara, 117

Guide, the, 8–10, 93–97, 109, 121–23, 125–26

Guru, the, 8–10, 37–39, 45, 59–60, 63–68, 91, 100–1, 109, 125–26

Hand of God, The, 67–68; *see also* Rodin

Hand of the Devil Holding Woman, The, 54–56; *see also* Rodin

Harmony, 72–73, 75, 79–80, 86, 122–23

Hope, *see* desire

Inclusivism, 107–9, 112–14, 133–34
Indeterminableness (of the relation between God and world), 118–19, 134
Institutions, religious, 3, 58–59, 80; as a continuity of seekers and teachers, 7, 69–71; as corrupt, 13–15; as an aspect of conventional religion, 20–21; as a harmony of spiritual pursuit, 75; as result and instrument of liberation, 84–85; and rejection of others, 97–98; *see also* Church, community

Jacob, patriarch, 47
Jesus of Nazareth: as teacher, vii, x, 5–7, 47–50, 77–78, 110–12; as Christ (Messiah), 2, 6, 10, 24–26; as divine Wisdom, 41–42; as savior, 44–45, 109; as both God and human being, 48–50, 119–20, 134; as God's gift of love, 70–71; "Farewell Discourse" of, 76–77; and attitudes toward outsiders, 111–14
John XXIII, Pope, 86
John Paul II, Pope, 4–5, 87, 116
John the Baptist, 5–6

Knitter, Paul, 108, 133
Koinonia, see communion

Liberation, *see* freedom
Lord's Supper, *see* Eucharist
Love, vii, 70–71, 75, 78

Man from Gandhara, 7–8
Matha, see Shringeri
Matrix, The, 55–56
Moment of Clarity, 16–17, 31–32
Mystery, 11, 60, 114–21, 134–35

Nirveda, see disgust
Nostra Aetate (Declaration on the Relation of the Church to Non-Christian Religions), 102–5, *see also* Vatican II

On Instructing the Uninstructed, 35, 70–71, 74–75, 119–20; *see also* Augustine of Hippo
On the Usefulness of Belief, 41–42; *see also* Augustine of Hippo

Paul, apostle, 31–32, 95
Peter, disciple, 24–27, 35, 110–13
Pine Ridge Reservation, 127–28
Pluralism, 108–9, 113–14, 133
Prasada, 38–39
Presence, personal, 46–47, 49–51
Priest, the, 8–10, 13–16, 35–36, 60, 91, 96, 102, 125–26
Professor, the, 1–2, 8–11, 91, 93, 125–26, 135
Promise, 76–81

Raft of knowledge, 68–69, 73–74, 83
Rahner, Karl, 107, 133–34
Ramakrishna Vedanta Society, 66–67
Religious, distinct from "spiritual," 2–4
Revelation, scriptural, 41–42, 56–57, 74–75
Risk, 26, 45–46, 49, 52, 59–60, 114
Rodin, Auguste, 54–55, 67–68

Samaritan woman, 47–50, 127
Santati, see continuity
Second Vatican Council, *see* Vatican II
Seekers, 6–7, 16–21, 23–24, 32–36, 40–42, 49–51, 68–69, 73–76, 85–86, 96–99, 105–6, 134–35
Self-knowledge, liberating, 7–8, 17, 56–57, 68–69; *see also* freedom

Shankaracharya, Adi: on the spiritual journey, 7–8; on the disciple's fitness for spiritual pursuit, 16–21, 40–41; on the qualifications of the teacher, 51–52, 57; on bondage and liberation, 56–57; on teaching lineage, 58–59; on the continuity of knowledge *(vidya-santati)*, 68–69; on the boat or raft of knowledge, 68–69, 73–74; on spiritual rebirth through knowledge, 82–84; on followers of other teaching traditions, 99–100; on the relation between God and world, 117–19

Shringeri, *matha* of, 64–66

Sisters of Mercy, 126–27

Social location, 130–31

Social justice, 3–5, 108, 128–29, 133

Spiritual, distinct from "religious," 2–4

Spirituality: of institutional commitment, 4–5, 96–97, 132–33; as socially conditioned, 34; as interior and exterior, 41–42; as analogous to friendship or

fluency, 46–47; as a shared pursuit, 68–69, 89–90

Synod of Bishops, Extraordinary (1985), 87–88

Teacher, The, 41, *see also* Augustine of Hippo

Teachers, 7–8, 36, 40–42, 46–61, 63–67, 73–74, 83–84

Thousand Teachings, A, 16–17, 37–38, 51–52, 56–57, 68–69, 73–74, 99, 117–19; *see also* Shankaracharya

Trust, *see* commitment

Tyagananda, Swami, 66–67

Upanishads, *see* Vedic scriptures

Vatican II, 86–87, 102–5, 115–16

Vedic scriptures, 7–8, 17–19, 51–52, 56–57, 82–83

Venerable Bede, 85

Wish-fulfillment, 28–29

Wood, Susan, 88–89

World Council of Churches, *see* Baar Statement

Index of Scripture References
(Hindu and Christian)

Chandogya Upanishad
6.14.1-2   7, 132

Law of Manu (*Manusmrti*)
2.144-50   x

Mundaka Upanishad
1.2.12-13   18

Genesis
1:26-27   68

Gospel of Matthew
12:46-50   81
16:17-19   25
18:20   69

Gospel of Mark
3:31-35   81
8:27-33   24–25

Gospel of Luke
3:1-2   6
8:21   81
9:18-22   25

Gospel of John
1:26   6
1:29   6
1:35-39   5
1:35-40   111
1:41   6
3:5   81
3:17-18   112
4:3-6   47
4:7-8   48
4:9a   48
4:10-26   48
4:17-18   49
4:27   48
4:28   49
4:39-42   50–51
10:14-16   113
13–17   76
13:1-38   76
13:12-15   vii
13:23-26   110
13:34-35   vii
14:1-3   113
15:1-27   76

16:1-15	76
17:17-23	77
20:29	50
21:15	111
21:16	111
21:17	111
21:19	111
21:20-22	110
21:24-25	110

Acts of the Apostles
2:44-47a	78

Letter of Paul to the Romans
7:21-25	31
13:13-14	32

Letter of Paul to the Philippians
2:6-8	119